PN Review 243

VOLUME 45　　NUMBER 1　　SEPTEMBER –

ON THE COVER
Stephen Chambers,
'State of the Nation I'
Credit: FS Photography

Editorial

AT UNIVERSITY IN 1968 I read the Penguin edition of Albert Camus's *Exile and the Kingdom* translated by Justin O'Brien, originally published a decade earlier. I was especially taken with the story 'Jonas, or the Artist at Work'. Wanting to read it again a year or two ago, I acquired a much later Penguin translation. The book was unrecognisable to me. Either memory played me false, or the gulf between the two versions was deep indeed. Half a century separated my readings and almost half a century stood between the two translations, with all the changes in language and custom entailed. Camus was alive when O'Brien published; indeed he was already at work when Camus received the Nobel Prize in 1957, the year the stories were first collected in France. O'Brien was a male translator; the later version was by Carol Cosman (2006).[1]

My Camus experience came to mind when I read Benjamin Moser's evaluation of Kate Briggs's *This Little Art* (Fitzcarraldo Editions, $20) in the *New York Times Book Review* of 1 July. His piece released a social media firestorm and provoked an orchestrated reply signed by nine of the little art's big guns, including Susan Bernofsky, Lydia Davis, Karen Emmerich and Lawrence Venuti.

I knew Moser as a re-translator of the Brazilian writer Clarice Lispector whose work featured in *PNR* in Giovanni Pontiero's translations in 1986 when Carcanet was publishing his versions of Lispector's major works. I did not warm to Moser's collaborative translations, but they cut the mustard with New Directions in New York and have been instrumental in re-establishing Lispector as a major feminist and modernist.

His review of Briggs, entitled 'Did He Really Say That? On the Perils and Pitfalls of Translation', I found bracing. He is a practitioner, a purist, and he is impatient with many of the nostrums of modern translation theory. Accustomed to the blistering precisions of Lispector, he is also piqued by some of the easier rhetorical gestures of contemporary essay writing. He engages with the techniques and tendencies of the book under review not piously but with the level of respect and self-respect one demands of a reviewer.

The review is accessible on the *NYTBR* website. I want to draw attention to points Moser makes which are pertinent if modern critical conversation is to continue as anything more than tenure track activity and that indulgent monologuing that allows translators and critics to behave like primary artists. This is not to say that their work is not very important (on the contrary), but its importance is, crucially, in relation.

Moser is unpersuaded early on. 'Kate Briggs's *This Little Art* is a meditation on translation, mainly derived from her experience translating two volumes of lectures by Roland Barthes. It is full of quotes [...], and of speculations about how translation interacts with, distorts and inten-

sifies reading: "This is a translation!" she writes, of her own book. "I feel sure that something would happen – some adjustment to your reading manner would be very likely to occur – if you were to hear me all of a sudden insisting that it is."' In this passage he not implausibly feels the effect of Barthes: 'his writing is as notable for fudging and preciosity as it is for insight, and Briggs shares with him a tendency to imprecise language: "We need translations," she writes. "The world, the English-speaking world, needs translations. Clearly and urgently it does; we do. And this has to be a compelling argument for doing them."' 'But', he says with exasperation, 'this is not an argument. It is an assertion, and Briggs misses the opportunity to examine it. What, exactly, is so clear and urgent about the need for translation? Who, here, is the "we" – middle-class English speakers? What kind of translations do we need: of what, by whom?' It is hard not to share with Moser a distrust of that ubiquitous 'we' that dragoons the reader into an unearned complicity.

Kate Briggs's lyrical essay mode lets her off a range of scholarly and critical responsibilities. Her champions speak of her 'lyrical, insightful and contrapuntally crafted meditations on the art of translation – intercut with responses to an impressive range of writers, thinkers and theorists, most notably Roland Barthes'. It would seem that she was writing poetry, or a sonata, or creating a collage, or all three, but not a critical meditation.

Moser stands up for his professions – editor, translator and writer (he does not call himself a critic) – and asks of Briggs's writing a respect for standards in translation and critical discourse. 'As a translator, I reject the suggestion that serious translators take such a lax view of standards. And as a translated author, I have seen my work misrepresented in other languages. I cannot speak for Thomas Mann, but I am surely not the only writer who finds distortion of my words a grave offense.'

The big guns collectively find the book 'fresh, stimulating and inspiriting, vital and rich'. Five heady blurb adjectives, afflatus in action. They praise the book's 'elegance, humility and foregrounding of intellectual curiosity'. This is the language of a committee letter. The writers predictably smear Moser, his 'general tone of condescension and occasional misogynistic sniping'. Male writers criticising female writers are always 'misogynistic' nowadays. His is a 'simplistic and retrograde (Nabokovian?) insistence on accuracy as a universally determinable gold standard for translation', which professionals dismiss as obsolete. How can a translator be an artist if she or he must also adhere to standards of accuracy?

Moser's principal error is to try to detect and respond to Briggs's 'argument'. This is, apparently, not a proper goal for a contemporary critic. On the contrary, her advocates insist, she offers no continuous argument, no grand theory. 'Rather, contemplating personal and public histories of translation in the tradition of Montaigne's *essai*, and "actively parrying against the all-purpose explanation," she explores the forms of creativity and critical

---

1 An excellent Enithamon Press edition translated by Hilary Davies was published in 2016.

thinking, responsibility and risk inherent in every act of translation.' They address the *tone* of Moser's review which, they say, 'suggests that allowing for uncertainty, acknowledging complication and contradiction, including – and thinking with – "subjective impressions" (which he sets in opposition to "objective scholarship") implies a lack of argumentative rigor or intellectual seriousness.' This is tone of the most articulate kind, and a tone some readers may find congenial.

Moser represents 'the prevalent general misunderstanding of translation as a "concrete art"', they say, and he 'aids in the vilification and dismissal not only of Briggs but of translation itself along with translators, in a way that has consequences for what and how we read'. The Moser review I read was not 'perfunctory and dismissive' but sharp, principled and common-sensical. It took a book seriously. It did not suggest that it was not worth reading, only that it could have been better thought and written.

Cover Story

Stephen Chambers, 'State of the Nation 1'

THE IMAGE ON THE COVER by Stephen Chambers comes from one of three large and mysteriously dramatic landscape paintings that go under the collective title 'State of the Nation'. What these depict is a state of crisis, showing three versions of a pony express rider in the process of being pitched from his saddle, hat and mailbag flying. His path is strewn with sticks, obviously cut to length but not finished off, and so halfway between a state of natural growth and something fit for purpose, although what purpose is not clear. In two of the paintings, sticks are also seen in the messenger's grasp, like olive branches divested of their leaves, while the stick in the third painting has slipped from his hand and is flying through the air. In all three paintings, the urgency of the message is proportionate to the risk of its not being delivered. And a message of sorts is also expressed by the speech bubble that issues from the rider's lips. This speech is wordless, taking the form of a rainbow of different colours, suggesting that the state of the nation should relate to its being diverse in meaning, identity and purpose: a 'rainbow nation'.

Rod Mengham

News & Notes

Blasphemy and obscenity · Anthony Burgess moved to Malta in 1968. There, the authorities seized nearly fifty 'indecent' books from his luggage and destroyed them. They included novels by Angela Carter, Kingsley Amis and D. H. Lawrence. Fifty years later, at the International Anthony Burgess Centre in Manchester, the collection has been reconstituted in an exhibition 'which looks more widely at the themes of obscenity and censorship' and includes unpublished manuscripts and letters, audio recordings, and photographs by Anthony and Liana Burgess. Burgess was a foe of censorship of all kinds, including blasphemy and obscenity. His position might not pass muster today: this exhibition is a welcome provocation at a time when a new Savonarolism may be gathering force.

Politically necessary · In June, a twenty-three-year-old of the Driftpile Cree Nation in Alberta won the Canadian portion of the Griffin Prize for *This Wound is a World*, published by Frontenac House. Billy-Ray Belcourt is reported to have sobbed as he accepted the $65,000 Griffin Poetry Prize. He is the youngest recipient ever of the prize. 'This book was written not to be a book,' he said. 'It was written [...] to allow me to figure out how

to be in a world that I did not want, a world that many of us who are Indigenous did not want. It was written also to try to bring about the world that we do want collectively.' Interviewed, he spoke of the prize as an 'investment' in 'the voices of all people like him who are Indigenous, queer or gender non-conforming [...] This is a siren call from the future.' As always with the Griffin, politics were an important ingredient in the decision. The three-member jury called the book 'politically necessary'. The international winner of the Griffin, also pocketing $65,000, was the American poet Susan Howe, for *Debths*, published by New Directions.

Power and Verve · *from the Bloodaxe website*: 'Matthew Sweeney was born in Lifford, Co. Donegal, Ireland in 1952. He moved to London in 1973 and studied at the Polytechnic of North London and the University of Freiburg. He established his literary reputation while based in London over two decades, becoming as well known in Britain – where he was always published – as in Ireland. Theo Dorgan described him as 'one of the finest poets of his generation, a craftsman of the highest achievement, with a distinct music all his own. More than this, though, and from the start, he had the courage of his own idiosyncratic sensibility; nobody now writing has Matthew's gift for employing the language and images of fable to such dark and unsettling effect, ringing the changes from tenderness to dark comedy with such power and verve.' The editors of *PNR* are honoured to publish four of his poems in this issue (pp.38–9).

Mighty poet · Donald Hall was a major poet and man of letters. He died in June, just short of his ninetieth birthday. He was the American poet laureate from 2006 to 2007, characterised as the 'laureate of rural life', a member of the American Academy of Arts and Letters. He received the National Medal of the Arts. *Poetry* magazine editor Don Share wrote that his work 'ran the gamut of human feeling, but he expressed emotions from joy to sorrow with a formal wit that has never been excelled, or even matched, in American poetry'. Death elicits large claims for the deceased, as though they might still be in earshot.

He was a significant presence in British poetry for many years as well, introducing American writers as critic and anthologist and engaging with the British main stream, writing in these pages on Frost, Gunn and others between 1976 and 1997, and contributing poems. In his later years his attention, and attention to him, was principally American. He became the New England poet par excellence, following Frost's footsteps. His poems are more a commemorative, measuring loss rather than endurance and survival, though he survived cancer in 1989. From 1975 until his death he lived in a farmhouse his family had occupied for generations, and in which he had spent his holidays as a boy ('coming home to the place of language'); he had a deep feeling for the informing traditions that were ebbing away all his life. He was married for twenty-three years, until her death in 1995, to the remarkable poet Jane Kenyon, and he elegised her in two books.

He wrote copiously, inexhaustibly: poetry, criticism, memoir. He was proud to have evaded the academy, although he did write textbooks, which helped to butter his bread. He made his living as a writer (of, among other things, children's books and books about baseball) and anthologist. His Penguin *Contemporary American Poetry* (1962, revised 1988) was the main route into American poetry for two or more generations of British readers.

His last contribution to *PN Review* was the poem 'Mighty Poets'. It begins:

When I asked Wallace
Stevens' permission to reprint poems
    he published in the *Advocate*,
he acceded with a note
    that set me thinking: 'Some
of one's early things give one the creeps.'
    Later I went up to him
at a brunch before The Game, where
    he stood with friends
from Hartford Accident and Indemnity.
    I deferred to the poet;
the businessman blushed and muttered.
    I asked if he could stay
in town through Monday; the *Advocate*
    was giving a party
for Mr Eliot - 'or maybe

for you both?' 'Shit,' he said,
'fuck. Got to get back to the office.'

Lewisiana · Patrick Worsnip writes: Cyril 'Cy' Fox, the Canadian journalist who was also a leading authority on Wyndham Lewis, well-known to long-term readers of this journal as a feisty contributor from 1978 to 2007, died suddenly on 10 July, just short of his eighty-seventh birthday, in St John's, Newfoundland, the city where he was born. He studied law at Oxford under a Rhodes Scholarship in the 1950s, then completed a Masters in modern history at Columbia, New York, before joining the Associated Press news agency in 1961. Two years later he moved to Canadian Press, transferring to London in 1967. From there he covered a range of foreign stories including the Paris student riots, the troubles in Northern Ireland and the Turkish invasion of Cyprus. He joined Reuters in 1974 as a chief sub-editor in London. Though regarded by some of his colleagues there as an eccentric, as a Reuters reporter whose stories he often worked on, I remember him as an excellent editor. When you saw the initials C. J. F. at the bottom of your story, you knew it would have been well handled. Cy retired in 1986 and returned to Canada in 1994 after his health began to suffer from 'years of relishing English beer in Fleet Street pubs'.

His main legacy is his work on Lewis, the non-conformist British writer and artist at the centre of Vorticism, a short-lived modernist art movement of geometric abstraction which grew out of Cubism and Futurism in the First World War era. Cy amassed the world's most comprehensive collection of Lewisiana – around nine hundred books, art works, magazine clippings, tape recordings, correspondence and other items - and became a world authority, corresponding, reading, lecturing and writing about Lewis. He had no idea what his collection was worth. Wherever he went, he rummaged around bookshops and snapped up anything Lewis-related. After half a century of this activity, in 2006 he donated it to the library at the University of Victoria, British Columbia, where it is held in a special collections vault. When movers hauled away the last box from his then home in Toronto, he was bereft. 'It left me limp. A huge void. A huge gap,' he said. 'I was seized by this character and he has never let go,' Cy once told an interviewer. 'He's still there up on the bookcase, ready to start talking. As soon as I open the page I hear that voice ready to bark out at you in the most spirited fashion. Very amusing, too. Entertaining. Very outspoken. Very honest. Direct. Exciting in the extreme.'

Counter to the grain · John Murphy writes: The poet Macdara Woods has died, aged seventy-six. He was a founding editor of *Cyphers* along with Eiléan Ní Chuilleanáin (to whom he was married), Pearse Hutchinson and Leland Bardwell. James Liddy said of the *Selected Poems* (Dedalus Press), 'This poetry has run counter to the grain. It is lush, surreal, linguistically rhetorical. This is not a domesticated poetry, the kitchen doesn't unravel its somnolent marvels here [...].' The poet Gerard Smyth, remembering him in the *Irish Times*, said, 'he was very much wedded to place and identifiably so in his Dublin poems, specifically those located on home ground in Ranelagh, to which he returned again and again with inventive poetic success.' Many younger Irish poets will remember him as someone who published (with his co-editors) their first poems in *Cyphers*, and who gave new poets the benefit of his kind, precise, unforgettable encouragement at the magazine's launch readings. He was joint-winner (with Mary O'Malley) of the 2018 Michael Hartnett Poetry Award for *Music from the Big Tent* (Dedalus Press).

Good modernist practice · Adam Piette writes: *Blackbox Manifold* [http://www.manifold.group.shef.ac.uk/] launched its twentieth issue in July, marking ten years of poetry publishing. Editors Alex Houen and I are pleased to have made it so far, and to have played a part in publishing exciting work by a range of poets from across the world. *Blackbox Manifold* started when we were colleagues at the University of Sheffield: we thought we would have a shot at editing a poetry journal, and decided on four things: to keep it simple and publish online; to have a two-editor selection process which meant we both had to like the work for it to pass; to mix up the best of mainstream-modernist work with experimental poetry; and to encourage submissions of poetic sequences and prose poetry.

The decision to go for online was not simply for pragmatic reasons: it seemed timely to do so, with technological changes making dissemination, editing and mixed media presentation possible, and also making the ambition to reach an international audience plausible. We were drawn to the success of *Jacket* magazine, in particular for its breadth, global scope and sustained presence.

The two editor rule was a rational one: it meant that taste might more confidently act as discrimination: we could both share our strengths and different preferences, but also distinguish blind spots, follow hunches, take risks more readily. For the most part we share views about the quality of work submitted, and have become increasingly confident that the editing process is not gatekeeper-authoritarian but genuinely supportive of good work. We commissioned work from poets we admired in the early stages, and are grateful to the poets who helped us; and also to those who have helped us as associates to the project, including Agi Lehoczky, Vahni Capildeo, Geraldine Monk, Alan Halsey, Sam Ladkin and many others.

The journal has done something to encourage narrative poetics, and our special sections on translation and sequences, and commemorative tributes to Tom Raworth and others, have also added variety to the claim we made from the beginning: we were looking for good work across the ordinary divide between experimental and mainstream, to encourage good modernist practice, and also to respond to the new generation of poets coming through in the UK, Australia, the Caribbean, the United States and elsewhere who are making different networks and groupings possible. We do not believe online journals harm the job done by those producing material chapbooks, books, pamphlets and anthologies; the world of poetry is big enough to sustain a variety of forms and formats. The ease of online dissemination does help poets, we believe, spread their words: we hope *Blackbox*

Manifold will remain a prominent, enabling little magazine. With thanks to contributors and readers over the last twenty issues and ten years!

Icon of Guarani poetry · The Paraguay-born Carlos Abente, the 'icon of Guaraní poetry', died in Argentina at the age of one hundred and three; he would have turned one hundred and four in September. He lived in Argentina for almost a century. The president of the Society of Authors of Paraguay characterised him as 'poet and philanthropist'. He was a doctor by profession, one of a group of Paraguayan exiles, bilingual in Spanish and Guaraní. His major work in Guaraní is the trilogy of poems beginning with *Che kiriri asapukái haguã*. He was also a significant poet in Spanish, but his work in Guaraní became well-known and popular due to musical settings by a variety of composers.

Prof Atukwei Okai · On 13 July *Modern Ghana* reported that the nation's 'iconic poet Prof Atukwei Okai' had died. He was the Secretary-General of the Pan African Writers Association of Ghana. The official statement reads: 'Prof Okai, 77, is noted for his excellent poetry recitation and is believed to be one of the first real poetry performers to have emerged in Africa.' He appeared at the now legendary 1975 Poetry International at the Queen Elizabeth Hall, London, where read with Stanley Kunitz, Robert Lowell and Nicolas Guillen of Cuba.

A Carcanet classic · John Heath-Stubbs is celebrated on 15 September at 2.30p.m. at St James' Church, Piccadilly, with a concert and reading of his work by friends and contemporaries. C. H. Sisson described him as a poet 'with a Miltonic disability' which he overcame with remarkable confidence, writing, teaching and travelling widely. John Clegg's new *Selected Poems of John Heath-Stubbs* will shortly feature in the Carcanet Classics list. It includes some of his celebrated Leopardi translations, much admired by Samuel Beckett. Peter Dickinson's *The Unicorns Suite*, dedicated to the poet, and taking its title from the opera they composed together, has its premier in 2019.

Marginalised classes · The Peruvian poet, philosopher, novelist, mathematician, dramatist artist and essayist Enrique Verástegui, a member (with Jorge Pimentel, Juan Ramírez Ruiz, Jorge Nájar, Enriqueta Belevan, and Carmen Ollé whom he later married) of the avant-garde Zero Hour Movement, a key poet in the 1970s generation, died in July at the age of sixty-eight. His first book, *En los extramuros del mundo*, published in 1971, was immediately recognised in Latin America. The Zero Hour movement (named after the magazine where its first manifesto appeared) was devoted to evolving a new, non-canonical poetry (though César Vallejo was honoured), a poetry close to daily life, to the 'marginalised classes', and to the harsh reality of modern Peru. He travelled widely, taught and wrote in Europe, but his focus was always on Peru and its culture. He wrote essays on all the significant Peruvian poets. His work is rooted in a rich culture, and because he was so securely grounded he was able to bring into play alien elements that much enriched his readers and fellow writers.

Earwormed by a Keynote, with Added Ghosts

VAHNI CAPILDEO

When A4 scrawlings unfolded one morning from disturbed storage, they found themselves transformed right there on their sheet into a gigantic inkstain. They were lying on there shelved, as it were grammar-plated back and did not bother fluttering up as they recalled having been divided into panels and bullet points. Apparently, poetry no longer kept to its place and was about to go down the chute. The numerous names which had been omitted from the bulk of the argument flickered like thin ghosts, powerless except in their resistance to exorcism.

This essay will attempt to metamorphose. Kafka is not the scriptwriter in the sky.

The A4 scrawlings were notes taken during Peter Riley's speech 'What Happened to Poetry?'. This was the keynote at 'The Motley Muse', an event dedicated to poetry and creativity, hosted by Steve Ely at the University of Huddersfield. The respondent, Sandeep Parmar, and her substitute, Khadijah Ibrahim, were absent for unavoidable reasons. There followed a presentation by Brian Lewis, poet and co-founder of Longbarrow Press. 'The Edge of the Map' saw Lewis exploring Yorkshire locations on foot with poets and others, and sharing an array of the responses produced, including some dazzling book art that one longed to be able to take out of the two-dimensional projection and hold, paper topography to wonder at in the hand. The discussion came alive, with Emma Bolland and others raising questions about access, arguing for the journeying of the feminine, disabled, queer. Perhaps Yorkshire, with its killingly beautiful and varied landscape, and its history of industries and skills, and misgovernment by London, is at an unfair advantage when its writers want to go walking. Nothing could be further from southern English masculine flaneurs and their mutual hypnosis by litanies of *phosphorescent... eels... multi-storey... clitoris... electric... Tories... forcible... gin...*

Participants in 'The Motley Muse' included Ian Duhig, Clare Pollard, Chris McCabe (for our 'interdreaming' collaboration), Warda Yassin, Elise Unerman, Zaffar Kunial and Jay Bernard. The young poets of Hive South Yorkshire were a bright note, themselves and their words. Some events are programmed to include a durational activity that threads time together, for example a relay of poets doing continuous freewriting. In Huddersfield, the sound sculpture by Ryoko Akama created continuity, 'in situ all day'. There were enough breaks for people to visit the installation, and enough space to be aware of co-presence without intrusion or overlap. Overall, it was truly an excellent gathering, with hopes of more to come.

Where the place? Upon the heath. There to meet with... Here I have a critic's thumb, Wreck'd as homeward he did come... But wherefore could I not pronounce 'diverse'? I had most need of poets, and 'diverse' Stuck in my throat... Is this essay haunted? Not to say, possessed.

The keynote speech has earwormed me, despite the day's departures from it. It struck a silvery, amiable tone. Good fellowship sounded like wind chimes behind the words. Poetry in the twentieth century used to be one thing, and now is two things. We would not talk about diversity, because we all know about that. Poetry was specialised and without a public presence before the 1960s and the distraction of gigs. In the twentieth century, the sources of information about poetry were published criticism and anthologies. There were no... There were no... 'There were no...' became a structure, a refrain. With such lulling, ghosts invade...

This is London calling the West Indies... Shut up, Henry Swanzy. Get thee behind me, Una Marson. Don't mention the radio.

The radio was not mentioned.

The disturbance of Modernism which happened in the 1920s had been suppressed by the 1940s. There were plenty of women around. It is an illusion that there are more young and female poets nowadays; they are just noticed more. 'Poetry is not a cruise ship', does not consist of lists of 'exotic places and animals'.

An ink blot obscures the heavy jitterbug of my scrawl. *My dear Wormwood, I sometimes wonder whether you think you have been sent into the world for your own canonisation. I gather, not from your mellifluously partial report but from that of the Poetry Police, that the subjects' behaviour during the first raid has been the worst possible.* Screw that tape. We're not in Narnia any more.

To be fair, no geographical limit was set for the discussion of 'what happened to poetry'. As I listened to what was said, I tried to contain, in asterisked notes, what was not said. Unaccountable figures danced in these silenced edgelands of the real text of the talk. Here are some of them. Travellers are inconvenient; no less so the British writers and translators who often brought 'home' the 'exotic'; easier to leave them out, along with Commonwealth writers, for whom the 'exotic' was home, and they would keep mentioning it; easiest not to think of what it means that some people had the temerity to move back and forth between territories, upsetting the notion of the 'exotic' by populating their imagination all over the place. Strictly, even roses and nightingales should be suspect, having spread from Persia. Decolonisation is an ugly word. Questions like employment, leisure, access, violence, contraception, domesticity – power – do not arise. Certainly numerous young people and women, and young women, were around; unlike today, they did not do 'promotional sales talk'. There is no need to look at the contents page of anthologies or the mastheads of magazines and count up on one's fingers. There is no need to quote one single poem.

After such knowledge, what forgiveness?

As Sara Ahmed observes and analyzes, to be attuned to hear what is jarring, and to articulate that, is to risk being experienced as jarring. It is not easy to write about a speech given by a pleasant man in a pleasant tone. Like a manly psychogeographer, I hide behind my literary ghosts.

It jarred to hear those outwith the 'critical overview' termed as the 'unorthodox'. Are there not greater, and other, orthodoxies? There are regions where English-language lyrics are appreciated – judged – alongside Bengali or Tamil ones; the traditions intertwine. There are countries where poets, 'good' poets, 'page' poets, have fought with word and hand in the streets, a public arena, in the twentieth century. There are means of dissemination beyond anthology and magazine: old, broken and lost typewriters, shabby suitcases, stencils, graffiti on crumbled walls; under extreme conditions, memory and word of mouth. It jarred to hear that a themed festival makes for inauthenticity, for the curtailment of true choice. This disregards how the conditions under which supposedly individual poets write are anyway not free (precarious employment? insecure housing? bombardment by fake news? simple bombardment? illness from environmental hazards? surveillance by violent states? disenfranchisement of one's mother tongues? jail?). Further, it disrespects the strength of the poetic impulse to refashion any given focus. It jarred to hear that poetry has had to 'refer itself as an adjunct' to causes.

... play a nocturne using a drainpipe as a flute?

To conclude that what 'happened' to poetry is a shift towards 'quantifiable humanity' away from, or against, 'common humanity', is reprehensible. The sensibility of an Elsa Cross or A. K. Ramanujan or Mayakovsky does not decenter humanity. Yet how rude is this essay, written up from literal blots, in paraphrasing the conclusion as: 'White English masculine consciousness natural. Anything else unhomely. Nothing to learn (except the universal truths and natural laws administered by colonially-derived educational systems and big publishers). Anything else an effort, diversion or imposition.' Yet that is how the sweet tones struck my understanding.

Gentle tendentiousness deserves no pity, even for its fear that the old and sometimes valuable will be scrapped, to be replaced by the new and sometimes dubious. For we poets need to lose our post-imperial inheritance of erasures, sutures of expediency, and lies. For example, in the available materials, the exchanges of Middle Eastern thinkers with Europeans of medieval and early modern times have been whitewashed. Anglo-American writers are scarcely read or anthologized alongside their poetic correspondents in the global south as a matter of course. *The C Major of this life...*

The old is diverse, and continuous with the new, but its sound sculptures are partially drowned out. Whatever happened, poetry needs a different recovery, de- and re-installation.

Spit in the hole, man, and tune again.

At the Poetry Summit

NICHOLAS MURRAY

'The Season has been a very bad one for new Books,' John Clare's publisher John Taylor wrote to him *à propos* of *The Shepherd's Calendar*, published in 1827 and selling only four hundred copies by 1829, '& I am afraid the Time has passed away in which Poetry will answer... the Shepherd's Calendar has had comparatively no Sale... I think in future I shall confine my Speculations to works of Utility.'[1]

Nearly two hundred years later it seems that poetry's time has far from passed away according to statistics presented at the recent Poetry Summit at the London Book Fair organised by the Poetry Book Society/Inpress and National Poetry Day. Slide after slide from the book trade's leading experts confirmed that poetry sales last year overtook 'works of utility' – and indeed all other categories bar 'politics and government' – to show the highest percentage growth in the entire book business. Talk of a poetry boom can no longer be contradicted if the evidence is its aggregate sales figures.

The Nielsen Bookscan pie chart confirmed that in 2017 poetry sales were worth 38.2 million and had increased in volume by 38.8%. Oliver Mantell of The Audience Agency, although conceding that there has been 'very little research on the consumption of poetry' asserted that 3.1% of the population claims to have written poetry in the last twelve months. That's 1.4 million people. André Breedt of Nielsen added that, with one hundred and thirty eight poetry venues and three thousand and eighty-one poetry events put on last year nationwide, the value of sales in the 'sector' is three million pounds.

Powerpoint slides talk in headlines and the critical question of which poetry sells and which doesn't needs a far more precise answer. Breedt's reference to 'that Homer book' – E. V. Rieu's enduring translation of the *Odyssey*, the first ever Penguin classic, and in its revised 2003 edition still seeing off all rivals – indicates that there is poetry and *poetry*, and that classics and anthologies are where the big sales are rather than in the traditional slim volume of verse. Hard data on individual collections is seldom disclosed – one poetry publisher recently told me that sales of new books could range from ninety-two copies to over seven thousand but I am aware of no more systematic research into the sales of serious poetry. It seems counter-intuitive to argue that such poetry is matching the sales boom typified by Rupi Kaur, the poet who launched herself on Instagram and now sells in millions.

Performance poetry, with its emphasis on audiences and the live event, attracts crowds and followers, appeals to booksellers (witness the tottering piles of Rupi Kaur in all the high street book chains) and generates a pop-concert level of interest which unsurprisingly translates into sales in the way that a discreet reading over a pub in a small market town could never aspire to.

Book fairs and data analyses are about numbers and the questions that will preoccupy serious poetry readers are seldom if ever about figures. The Poetry Summit in the end was an event where quantity was the issue not quality and the hyperbolic language of marketing – like the noisy groupthink of the social media, where acclamation has largely driven out criticism – is in a different register from the language of discriminating criticism.

Sitting in the hall at the London Book Fair where the summit was taking place, I struggled to connect all the excitement over sales with my own experience as a tiny independent poetry pamphlet publisher, Rack Press. The average print run of one of our poetry pamphlets that might attract excellent reviews in the literary papers or win one of the many awards for poetry is around one

---

1 Introduction by Eric Robinson and Geoffrey Summerfield to *The Shepherd's Calendar*, John Clare (1964), p.vii.

hundred and fifty. Sometimes that can be exceeded, even doubled, if the poet is good at marketing, has lots of readings, a forceful personality (a euphemism for being good at twisting people's arms before they escape from the gig) or lots of friends. There are some excellent bookshops – like the London Review Bookshop – with well-stocked shelves and well-informed booksellers but even they cannot, I would guess, claim substantially higher sales for some of those slim volumes.

The poetry editor of Penguin recently asserted that we are currently living through a Golden Age of poetry. Certainly poetry is making more noise. More people are writing, and maybe even reading it. Poets are pouring off the creative writing courses and naturally looking for publishers, the result of which is that many small publishers like Rack Press have had to close their doors to new submissions to avoid being drowned by them. Adjudicating on the claim that this is a Golden Age will depend on one's sense of what good poetry is and on the values of those who are the gatekeepers: the publishers, critics, reviewers, festival organisers, awarders of prizes and bursaries. I am not sure this is a question that can, in the end, be resolved by statistics for it is a matter of taste.

One doesn't want to sound negative. There is much that can be done to help sales (and all publishers want to sell their wares) particularly through supporting small independent publishers who still take many of the biggest risks though, arguably, they have less to lose and can afford to take chances. There are still at present many obstacles for us to overcome. Rack Press for example is too small even for independent press promotion outfits like Inpress. We are excluded from the annual Forward Prize jamboree, which refuses to look at pamphlets, even the new poems within them which are thus barred from the Best Single Poem contest. We lack sales teams, and feet in the door up and down the country and therefore struggle often to let the world know of our riches. I can think of practical measures that could be of assistance. For example, could not the Arts Council and other bodies fund a team of experienced sales representatives to work one day a week exclusively for the small poetry presses? No handouts, just a bit of useful free legwork.

And reviews would help, and have helped us. Many valuable new full-length collections, from much larger publishers than we are, attract no reviews at all. I sympathise with review editors who must struggle to choose which new collections to send out to reviewers and one consequence of a putative boom is that rare and interesting voices are more likely to be unheard in the general din. The patient work of finding the poetry that truly matters goes on.

As an undergraduate English student in the 1970s at Liverpool University my head of department, the great Shakespeare scholar Kenneth Muir, once told me that as an undergraduate at Oxford in the 1930s he had joined a queue outside Blackwell's for the latest slim volume from Auden, a queue which stretched away down the street and around the corner. Could that, he said with high professorial acerbity, happen today? Could it – boom or no boom – happen now?

I live in hope that it could.

Letter from Wales

SAM ADAMS

Meic Stephens has died at his home in Whitchurch, Cardiff, a few weeks short of his eightieth birthday. He was probably the most influential figure in the literary life of Wales in the second half of the twentieth century. A prodigious worker, he was constantly bringing forth fresh projects and restlessly digging at them until they were done, even into his last year. He was a *stakhanovite*, a term (learned in visits to Russia) he enjoyed using, though not in self-regard.

When I returned to south Wales in 1966 to take up a lectureship at what was then Caerleon College of Education, a fellow member of staff, Gwilym Rees Hughes, Welsh editor of the infant *Poetry Wales*, encouraged me to contribute to the magazine and soon after introduced me to Meic. Our friendship began at once and lasted. He and I were contemporaries at UCW Aberystwyth, though I was a few years ahead of him and did not get to know him there. Like many another hopeful English scholar, Meic was felled by Professor Gwyn Jones's Anglo-Saxon axe and pursued honours French instead. He had the better deal, for French was a gateway to a lasting interest in other cultures and languages. More immediately, as a newly qualified teacher, in 1962 it brought him a job at Ebbw Vale Grammar School. He was still wondering how he would get to Ebbw Vale daily, when an extraordinary serendipitous event occurred. While enjoying a pint at the Old Arcade, a venerable hostelry in Cardiff, which still at that time had little flaring gas jets near counter height where wealthier customers could light their cigars, he fell to talking with a stranger. They found they had much in common: Meic's French matched his Romance Languages at Oxford, and both were poets and staunchly Welsh Nationalist. So wrapped up were they in conversation they did not notice a gas jet burning a hole in Meic's coat sleeve. When the alarm was raised, the new acquaintance doused the minor conflagration with his pint of Guinness. It was one of those curious turning-points at which the direction of a life changes.

The fellow drinker, Harri Webb, was inviting others of similar cultural tastes and political leanings to join him in a large house at Merthyr Tydfil once owned by an iron-master. It was conveniently near Ebbw Vale, space was available at the top of the house and, since ownership of the property was uncertain, no one came to collect the rent. These were persuasive arguments: Meic joined the group at Garth Newydd. Soon, Radio Free Wales, a pirate radio station, was broadcasting from his room to a few neighbouring Merthyr streets, while downstairs Harri was editing *Welsh Nation*, Plaid Cymru's newspaper. Working alongside Harri, Meic learned essential editorial skills and in 1963 he launched his own publishing imprint, Triskel Press. It was under this banner that the first number of *Poetry Wales* appeared in 1965, price three shillings. The print run of five hundred copies cost forty-seven pounds and the editor doubled as salesman: it was a sell-out.

A survey of the contents pages of early numbers of the magazine reveals the vital part it played in what Meic was to term 'the second flowering' of Anglo-Welsh writing (as it was then known), the first flowering having occurred in the 1930s. At once we meet Roland Mathias, Harri Webb, Sally Roberts, John Tripp, Anthony Conran, Leslie Norris, Dannie Abse, Raymond Garlick, John Ormond, Vernon Watkins, R. S. Thomas and more, all poets who would make their mark in the decades that followed, in the 1970s, alongside the emerging new generation, including Gillian Clarke and Robert Minhinnick. Among other features of the magazine that had a lasting impact was the appearance of Welsh-language poets in the same lists, an early expression of Meic's bridge-building between the two language traditions, and the space and prominence given to articles and reviews of poetry publications.

Throughout this time he was also a political activist on behalf of Plaid. To him, mixing literature and politics was not problematic, though he would not have earned himself any credit in the Labour heartlands of south-east Wales, especially after being caught 'white-handed', as he says in his autobiography, *My Shoulder to the Wheel* (2015), daubing the words 'Lift the TV ban on Plaid Cymru' on the wall of Cyfarthfa Castle, and fined twelve pounds by the Merthyr magistrates. He participated in the early campaigns of Cymdeithas yr Iaith (the Welsh Language Society), and was justly proud to have been photographed in February 1963 among the crowd of young people who blocked traffic on Trefechan Bridge, the main road into Aberystwyth from the south. About the same time he added the graffito 'Cofiwch Tryweryn' to a wall near Llanrhystud, which, having been refreshed by others over the years, has become a patriotic rallying cry. Involvement first as agent for the Plaid candidate for Merthyr at the 1964 General Election, then as candidate himself in the 1966 election, brought nothing but lost deposits. It put him off a career in politics, for which the Muse is grateful, but there was an unexpected bonus. He met his future wife, Ruth Meredith, a co-worker, in 1964. Their marriage in August 1965 drew him into a large circle of men and women prominent in contemporary Welsh life. He had begun learning Welsh during teacher training at UCNW Bangor and Welsh became and remained the language of their home, which in August 1966 was in Rhiwbina, a Cardiff suburb. It was there I think I met him and quite soon after joined him on *Poetry Wales* as reviews editor.

Meic had left teaching to become a reporter with the *Western Mail*. A year later, in September 1967, he was appointed to what was soon after redesignated the Welsh Arts Council and his post within it Literature Director. In addition to an unusually wide familiarity with contemporary writers and writing in Wales, the appointing panel must have seen in him the fire in the belly, the enormous appetite for work and the will to get things done. It was no wonder he could be impatient with those who were less alert and energetic, and that he made enemies during his twenty-three years in the role. Aspiring writers whose applications for grant aid were turned down by the Literature Committee tended to blame him as the figurehead. They were far outnumbered by friends and admirers who appreciated his efforts to promote the culture of the English-speaking Welsh and to build bridges between Welsh- and English-language writers. Much of the achievement in raising the ambitions and standards of writers and critics in Wales, and the quality of book production, can be traced back to him and his productive relationships with a succession of committee chairmen, notably Glyn Tegai Hughes, Roland Mathias, Walford Davies and M. Wynn Thomas. So evident was the worth of several literary initiatives pioneered in Wales that they were adopted by the other UK arts councils.

One might have thought he had enough on his plate, but he also contrived to maintain a high level of activity as writer and editor. As an undergraduate he had seen himself as a poet rooted in industrial south Wales, and was influential as such, but he was not prolific and published little in the English language after *Exiles All* (1973). In later years, however, on several occasions he came close to winning the Crown at the National Eisteddfod for poem sequences in Welsh, his third language. *Linguistic Minorities in Western Europe* (1976) revealed the depth of his interest in the rich diversity of languages and cultures, and again in later years he published translations from Welsh and French. He was an inveterate and orderly collector of quotations and information on literary topics and, above all perhaps, he will be remembered for his scholarship and his remarkable gifts as compiler and editor. These were demonstrated in numerous publications, most notably in his joint editorship (with Dorothy Eagle) of the *Oxford Illustrated Literary Guide to Great Britain and Ireland* (1992), and his crowning achievement, the *Oxford Companion to the Literature of Wales* (1986), which was also published in Welsh and subsequently in enlarged and updated editions.

He left WAC to freelance but soon found himself Professor of Welsh Writing in English at the University of Glamorgan. When, in 2006, he retired from that position, if leisure beckoned he dismissed it with a sharp kick. More important big books followed, among them: *Poetry 1900–2000* (2007), *Rhys Davies: A Writer's Life* (2014), which won Wales Book of the Year, and (jointly edited with Gwyn Griffiths) *The Old Red Tongue* (2017), a monumental anthology of Welsh literature. I was very fortunate to have known Meic as a friend for approaching fifty years. We sent drafts of work in progress to one another for comment, we recommended and exchanged books, we worked together on the Rhys Davies Trust, which Meic founded in 1990. We spoke often and at length on the telephone, rarely without laughter at the vagaries of the world.

Presencing the Bright Particulars

From The Journals

R. F. LANGLEY

23 JANUARY 2007

Sun and blue sky. Winter sun. It has been cold; there is crushed ice on some puddles. In Edwards' Lane, on the bank which catches the warmth, small red nettles have flowers, as do a speedwell and a white nettle. There are leaves of arum and buttercup. Earlier, in the church,[1] I was stepping up the chancel looking at the back of Mr Coke's head up on the wall, when a dog barked from across the road, from down opposite the public house,[2] and the bark, a light one, sounded closer than it must have been. A marble statue, sunshine in a church, a dog barking... for some reason I received a momentary sense of a summer years ago, on one of our holidays in these parts, distinctly, a mental taste as it were. Marble in bright sun. Dog bark. I can fetch it back now, a touch of discovery, of wandering through the country lanes, of companions, of coming at the good statue from an angle. Mostly of the sunlight inside the building.

I pass from thinking about Wallace Stevens to thinking of Carlos Williams,[3] the presencing of the bright particulars, which begin to awaken, brown weeds, pallid or dull green weeds, the nettles with striped stems and a leaf, or several, at their tops, held aloft. The mash of dead leaves cleared off the asphalt now, swept close in under the verges so the road feels cleaned... By the road, under the surge of blue, the white cumulus driven from the northeast, the upstanding stuff, twiggy.

The dry, pale marble head facing away from me in the new sunshine. A dog barking. A village outside. Come here to see. And then, later, the question of what sources this happiness, what does it lead to and stem from? Space, in time and place. The sense of here. Found in the autonomy of travel. Finding the memorably excellent in fine places. That there is quality and one has discovered it. That it is in country places, with plants and birds and weather and seasons, and has been for many years, hundreds of years, with people around all that time who noticed it also. So?

Then it seems hard to drive it deeper, find further roots. Maybe it just swings round and back to the stone in the sun itself again, in the sun and the sound of the dog's bark, so that it is present. Yes. Not traded off or to be mastered. Just found in its place with my having enough knowledge and experience to place it, help it to presence in the advantage of the moment. As in a poem. To see it in there.

The flint axe becomes a work when its knapping, its knapped shape, does not disappear into the practicality of being an axe. Then it presences. Then you know Solutrean.[4] As do the weeds on the verge when they are more than the registration of the season, the forward spring, the content of chat, but, uncrafted as they are, they seem, I suppose, craft and their leafiness is glimpsed, as leaves. These leaves. Words as words when they are found in a poem. These words.

Further round the lane the field of young growth, glassy, is all shaking in the wind to far away, up the slope to the top against the sky, and up there a white cumulus cloud bulges over the rim, more steady and consolidated than the ground shivering below it. When, over the pasture's edge, the sea rises like a plant, restlessness and stillness transposed, present earth and sky, crop and cloud, in new essentials.

Then the white-haired man, trudging wide-legged back up the main road into the street, is Peter Farmer, though I can't be sure of this at first being blinded by low sun. After his operation he is finding walking hard, coming back from the shop along the Low Road, and I slow down to walk with him, to go with him home where Jean gives me coffee and biscuits. Peter can't walk further than the railway bridge up Edwards' Lane. He feels he will never be able to do more than that. There were bullfinches in the trees round the Folly, I tell him. He hasn't seen one for years. There used to be many before the orchards were grubbed up. But, I think, there are, nevertheless, a lot (of birds) between here and the railway bridge, some of which some time, could be bullfinches. Which you might happen upon.

Now, as I write this down, nudged chiefly by Coke's head, sunshine, the barking dog, it is half-past four in the afternoon in our bedroom and the sun has dropped, there being rosy cloud to the north through black motionless branches and Marie Woolley in a glowing orange coat on the field outside the south window, the lifted elbow, the stoop. Now she is forking hay. B is out in the car visiting a friend. The world holds on as low light stands into hedges and colours purplish, upstanding twiggy stuff of bushes out there and there is a greenish light on in one of the upper windows of the school, a prickle through branches.

When things seem more than what can be found to say about them. So you can indicate but not define. Which can't be invented, cannot be invented. You can tell at once if it has the easy viability or the easy cleverness of invention. It is inexplicable on the Internet, nor is it at all surreal.

---

1 St Andrew's Church, Bramfield, Nr Halesworth, Suffolk Memorial monument in black and white marble to Arthur Coke and his wife Elizabeth, 1634, by Nicholas Stone. He is higher on the wall, 'kneeling in armour; a stern man it seems' above Elizabeth who is 'represented comfortably recumbent... holding a baby... Extremely progressive for its date'. (Nikolaus Pevsner, revised by Enid Radcliffe, *The Buildings of England: Suffolk*, Penguin Books, 1974). The Cokes and this important sculpture feature centrally in R. F. Langley's poem *The Ecstasy Inventories*, pub. in *Hem*, 1978, and then in three later collections, as well as in many other more extended descriptions in his journals. A photograph of some of the carved hem on Mrs Coke's gown is the frontispiece of his *Complete Poems*, pub Carcanet Press, 2015.

2 Queen's Head, Bramfield.

3 Words, phrase and ideas from Carlos Williams' poems 'By the Road to the Contagious Hospital' and 'By the Edge of the Sea' are woven into this extract from here on.

---

4 The Solutrean industry is a relatively advanced knapped flint tool-making industry of the Upper Paleolithic era, from around 22,000 to 17,000 BP, named after the archaeological site at the Rock of Solutré, near Macon, Burgundy, France.

Now the rosiness has seeped up into the blue grey and we have cobalt magenta. And the light seeped into the scruff and pelt and nap of things, of a grass field, an asphalt road which is Bridge Street, verge and hedge, so that they all declare themselves present and adjacent. Nothing points away or leads you off. You are stuck against this, which is impossible to say. The infinite fine line of a telephone cable. The forked fork of the fork of a branch. Darkening sky replete with emptiness. Remaining light dawned on the rendered gable of a cottage in afterglow.

[edited by Barbara Langley, 29 June 2018]

---

from The Notebooks of Arcangelo Riffis

MARIUS KOCIEJOWSKI

15 March, 8.21 p.m. Mild. Many of the young women here have an odd & disagreeable habit of cutting men who approach them to ask directions. An hour ago, well-warmed with Burgundy & spleen I walked out of La T_e and met a girl coming in. Wanting to find a box to mail a letter to my Dutch friend in London, I approached her to ask if she knew where I could find one. She cut me & started toward the stairs. This whole miserable month snapped inside me, and I started after her down the hall; I grabbed her right arm, swung her around, and struck her hard across the face. She fell at the foot of the stairs, did not scream... just a sharp, amazed cry. A rather pretty chick, she'll have a black eye tomorrow. How will she explain it? This solitude during the past months has been eating at what little balance & fortitude I have left. I've more reason now to be afraid for myself than any other time since 1963.

16 March, 6.22 a.m. Mild. That was one of the cheapest, most sordid things I've ever done – and I had the incredible lowness to smirk about it afterwards. There can be few more terrible things than to awake in the morning & immediately recall a disgraceful act of the night before. In Denver, and again in L.A., I fought & laid a fellow on the curb for doing almost exactly the same thing. I should have been kicked from pillar to post. I will frequent La T_e in hope of seeing her again, and shall not rest until I've apologised to the girl, and then shall not rest. I am a boor, a barbarian & a thug. I used to call myself 'a gentleman in spite of everything'. Gentleman, I'll choke on the word now.

Good Friday, 18 April 2014. Pergolesi's *Stabat Mater* plays as I write. Such music contains the world's violence. Within the confines of the Cappucinni Convent in Pozzuoli, Giovanni Battista Pergolesi, in his final days, completed the *Stabat*, entrusting the manuscript to his friend Francesco Feo, luckily for us because the composer's possessions were sold to cover the expenses of his burial in a common grave. We do not know exactly, only roughly, where he is buried. Pergolesi was only twenty-six when he died from the *tabe ettica* or tuberculosis. *Quando corpus morietur, fac, ut animae donetur paradisi gloria.*[1] There's no scandal attached to his name.

'A sharp, amazed cry': the setting down of those four words brings to mind Dostoevsky's description of Raskolnikov bringing down an axe over the old woman's head at which point, remember, she weakly defends her skull with her upraised hands. That was Dostoevsky's genius, to produce the small detail that *actualises* so that we might partake of Raskolnikov's crime. The visual image of those upraised hands finds its aural equivalent in *a sharp, amazed cry*. A murder would have been somehow viable. At least one can imagine some way back from there. A slap across the face is harder to erase. A man who kills carries his guilt to the grave. A man who slaps the face of a woman, or a child, carries with him something more powerful than guilt: *shame*. Shame is the stickiest of all the soul's contaminates. Only another woman or child can ever free him of it. Why did Arcangelo, most self-censorious of men, allow this passage to survive? I would have expected a jagged edge down the middle of the notebook. There are other instances where pages have been removed. More vexing, however, is the question of whether I should allow this passage to see the light of day. I had even contemplated removing the offending page for isn't it the duty of a loyal friend, which surely I was, to preserve the other from infamy? Other things I will have barred from these pages, so why not this? If I were to suppress it, though, would I not have betrayed something bigger than friendship? And is it not incumbent upon me to see to it that he be allowed a shot at redemption? Was not the whole of his existence aimed at such an outcome? *Resolve*, that's what he always said to me. *Resolve, resolve.*

*

Such news I have of the world, Arcangelo, is this. A thrush sings outside. A chirping sparrow would fit the bill more given the ancient Romans held sparrows to be psychopomps bearing away the souls of the dead, only what's one to do with the disconcerting matter of the sparrow population having quit London en masse? We spoke about this, remember. Could it be the city's run out of souls virtuous enough for the taking? Are the psychopomps on strike? Questions were raised in parliament as to where those sparrows got to. This was over a decade ago and still they haven't returned. That thrush out there, it will do. I would prefer a blackbird, mind you, although really it's just another kind of thrush. Its bargain basement song is worth more to me than even the nightingale's. An hour ago, I watched through the kitchen window a man going through a plastic bag left outside the vacated office building opposite. Suddenly he froze. It was the posture of one who might have just solved one of the world's great riddles. Maybe he'd found the god particle in a bag of refuse. He walked away, smiling at his good fortune, carrying a sleeveless LP, the sun glinting for just a second from its shiny black surface. I've been reading Robert Walser who may be the closest modernist literature has come to producing a holy fool. I disagree with those critics who say he was a chronicler of the inconsequential because what he did surely was to make everything of equal importance. A strange light envelops his prose. What else? What else? Syria is in flames.

---

1 'When my body dies, let my soul be given the glory of paradise' – *Stabat Mater.*

NEW WELSH REVIEW

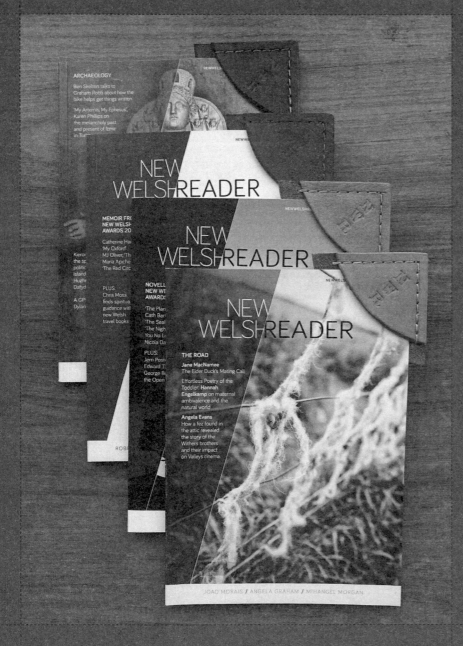

After Long Absence

John Ash

After long absence I found myself back,
all unwillingly, in the country of my sickness
where a kind nurse told me that the blue band
fastened to my wrist indicated 'cognitive impairment',
and I think there may be something to it. Why –

only yesterday I forgot how to spell
that grave word *catastrophe* when this
is what had happened like an unforeseen eclipse,
or shadow of an obliterating wing. In the hospital
as I waited to leave (and waited and waited)

to divert myself I read for the second time
Dame Freya's *Lycian Shore* and recalled
an ogival tomb standing in shallow water
amid tall reeds where a blue boat lay moored
beside the small forgotten town of Tristomon,

abandoned after plague. After infinite delays
I was wheeled out along an endless subterranean
corridor lined with ineffectual images of woodlands
and cathedrals – myself a minor Orpheus
or Theseus escaping underworld or labyrinth.

On emerging I saw what I had so quickly forgotten:
trees like clouds swaying as if drunk, and a sky
blue as the summer Marmara I had crossed so often
on ageing ferries heading for the islands of exile,
Yalova, and the promise of Asia.

Soon I would be home, or what passed for it
(for it was not mine) assuaged by music
after so many days of torpid silence in a high room
with a view of factories, power plants, stagnant waterways,
beautiful at night. In the taxi, gasping for breath,

overcome, I concluded that this was no time
to think of dying, and later as I lay, sleepless, a bird
began, on cue, to sing its tribute to the returning light.
Then silence returned like a recollection of menace,
and birch trees rustled against a sky white

as paper, this paper.

Poems

Yasser Khanjer & Fadwa Suleiman

Translated from the Arabic (Syria) by Marilyn Hacker

A Refugee

Yasser Khanjer

One day when I was little, my mother took me by the hand and said
We're going to fill a jug with water at the Spring of the Reeds.
And when we walk across those ruins
Hold on to the folds of my dress
And keep your eyes on the ground, son, to stay in step with me,
Follow the chime of my ankle-bracelets to find your way
If I'm gone for long, don't wait for me.
But remember – there is a sun holding its hand out to you gently
If your heart follows its path from that light
The path will lead towards dawn. Don't wait for me
You'll follow morning's chime on sleep under your eyelids
And the scent of roses on the bed of your stumbling childhood

*

Since I was little
A thread, unravelled from my mother's dress
Has been looped around my hand

Laurel

Fadwa Suleiman

I'm sitting alone in my room
my clothes scattered around me,

and my suitcase that took to the road with me when I fled

I keep telling it about our return, soon
You'll carry my clothes that crossed the border inside you when we go back
We'll walk on the streets, pass through the cities once more
We'll write on the ground with our own ink
and our ink to us will be attar and laurel

Like Armour

New Collected Poems by Marianne Moore, ed. Heather Cass-White (Faber & Faber, 2017) £30

JENA SCHMITT

WHILE READING *New Collected Poems* by Marianne Moore, edited by Heather Cass and published by Faber & Faber in 2017, I found myself making lists, lists of the people and places and things from within Moore's poems. First and foremost, there are animals – pigeons, buffalo, pelicans, basilisks, swans, nightingales, octopuses, snakes, mules, beavers, antelopes, pangolins. There are nectarines and plums, orchids and palm trees; views of Boston, Fujiyama, Thebes, Pompeii; references to Queen Elizabeth, Dante, Francis Bacon, Pliny, an elderly gentleman playing a game of chess.

I found entries in the index for carrots and Chinese lacquer, fools and Flaubert, marriage and manganese blue, waterfalls and Waterford glass. There are quotes from *Literary Digest*, *National Geographic*, *Field & Stream*, *Scientific American*.

Further, looking back through Moore's *Selected Letters* (1997), which I was lucky to find in a used bookstore more than twenty years ago, I noted the writers and artists she corresponded with – H. D., Elizabeth Bishop, Joseph Cornell, Alfred Stieglitz, Harriet Monroe, William Carlos Williams, Ezra Pound, T. S. Eliot, D. H. Lawrence, Wallace Stevens, W. H. Auden, Allen Ginsberg, Louise Bogan.

There were the nicknames she called her mother (most often Bear) and brother – Biter, Ouzel, Winks, Beaver, Pago, Pen-viper, Badger Volcanologist, Mongolian gazelle, Snowflea, Impala K. C. S. The names she called herself – Poisonous, Rusty Mongoose, Fangs, Uncle. The names – Weaz, Pidge, Winks, Rat (though most often Moore was Rat) – that she called all three of them, as though they were interchangeable, merely personae, or perhaps one formidable person. Moore lived with her mother most of her life, except while studying at Bryn Mawr College (1905–9), taking secretarial courses at Carlisle Commercial College (1910–11), and teaching bookkeeping, stenography, typing, commercial English and law at the Industrial Indian School at Carlisle until 1915, when she began to publish poems. She started living with her mother again in 1916, and they shared tiny apartments packed with books, knickknacks and other curios, first in New Jersey, then Greenwich Village, then Brooklyn, until her mother's death in 1947.

I had my own lists to make, of course, groceries to get, appointments to make or keep, books to read, important things to do, but found myself recording some of the lists Moore made instead. On 6 May 1909, Moore wrote to her mother and brother:

You asked me for a list of things I want:

Books, Whistler's *Ten O'Clock* and 'The Gentle Art of Making Enemies.'
Will Low's *Life of Saint-Gaudens.*
Swinburne (prose)
a rain coat
Pater
Book on Wagner's operas
[Henry Thornton] Wharton's *Sappho*
Xenophon's treatise on hunting
Watts' *Prometheus*
Botticelli's illustrations to *The Inferno*
Burne-Jones' *Paderewski*
[Thackeray's] *The Newcomes*
A bar pin on the order of '——' feather, Pleasance lost
The Oxford Book of Verse.
Chopin's waltz e sharp minor.

Though not exhaustive, these lists were funny and intriguing at first, then exhausting, a glimpse into Moore's eclectic interests, into her unyielding, wonder-filled mind.

I put *New Collected* aside and read other things, but references to Moore started appearing in the books I picked up. Poet Lucy Tunstall writes about 'the three-cornered, fuck-off / hat of Marianne Moore' in her collection *The Republic of the Husband*, while the perhaps overused 'What is more precise than precision? / Illusion' is an epigraph in *The Tragic Death of Eleanor Marx* by Tara Bergin. Finally, in *Dear Friend, from My Life I Write to You in Your Life*, novelist Yiyun Li writes:

> The contrast between writers' published work and private words makes one feel for them, but Moore's poetry and letters, equally opaque, close a door to anyone's curiosity. Perhaps my reading her is far from rebellion or intrusion. It is only to insist on being defeated. No one defeats better than Moore.

This might have been the point where I understood Li's gentle acceptance of Moore's forbearance, her discretion and protectiveness, of the walls she painstakingly built around herself and her work. Is that not what walls are for, after all? When Moore writes about 'the exteriorizing of the interior' in Bishop's poems, I can't help but think that Moore's poems are an interiorizing of the exterior, that there is a compactness, an exactness of phrase and detail that narrows closely in, then suddenly expands, shifting the ground underneath, the ceiling, the walls, a swiftness that is immediate and urgent, full of strange angles and dark corners. As if there were some imagined place she was trying to get to, or away from.

There are keenly felt omissions and sophisticated excesses, countless negative constructions, multiple multi-tonal voices, a strangely staged modesty, lines and syntax that crash into one another, line breaks ('ac- / cident – lack / of cornice, dynamite grooves, burns, and…') that feel as though they are actually breaking, an intertextuality as thick as a wool blanket. I started to see Moore as a study in opposites: light and dark, dated and contemporary, refined and ornate, clear and confounding, formal and experimental. There were battles going on, spaces you could fall through, look down toward, gaze up at. Not unlike Cornell's shadow-boxes, Moore constructed not only worlds, but worlds within worlds, as habitable as they are uninhabitable. Like a *mise en abyme*, the golden-hued mosaics in the Hagia Sophia, for instance, or a painting by Diego Velázquez or Giotto: rich, finely rendered, layered, darkly bright.

Her poems, at times, are loud menageries, at times refined, succinct affairs. Sometimes they fascinate, sometimes not. There are the enamouring 'gondoliering legs' of the swan in 'No Swan So Fine' and the description of a jellyfish in 'A Jellyfish':

Visible, invisible,
a fluctuating charm
an amber-tinctured amethyst
inhabits it, your arm

Or the cave-like echo in 'The Mind is an Enchanting Thing' 'is an enchanting thing'. There is also her wit, her sharpness in 'To Be Liked by You Would Be a Calamity' about an unwanted encounter, and 'Silence', the one poem where she talks about her father, who suffered a nervous breakdown before she was born and whom she never met:

My father used to say,
'Superior people never make long visits,
have to be shown Longfellow's grave
nor the glass flowers at Harvard…

The deepest feeling always shows itself in silence;
not in silence, but restraint.'
Nor was he insincere in saying, 'Make my house your inn.'
Inns are not residences.

Moore has a way of talking to the world while not talking to the world, of talking back, of withholding just enough ('omissions are not accidents', she famously wrote) so that the reader must put the pieces – mosaic- or collage-like – back together. These are the glass-sharp moments that easily prick the skin. If words could do such a thing.

But there is also the boredom of the animal poems, being that there are so many of them. *No more elephants or fish or porcupines or lemurs*, I couldn't help but think. There are poems such as 'Nine Nectarines and Other Porcelain', 'The Old Dominion', 'A Carriage from Sweden', 'The Jerboa' and 'The Hero' that make generalised, outdated comments about culture and race – 'theirs is a race', 'that choice race' – that come from a position of power and privilege, an 'other' that is ultimately damaging and racist.

It is in such defeats that we might learn the art of letting go. I set *New Collected Poems* aside again, which is, really, the point of a collected, to read, to wander away, to go back. There are moments when I like Moore and moments when I don't, moments that feel as exciting and original as when they were first written, others that have lost their lustre. Once we throw our hands up, we have the chance to stop, really stop and observe, press an ear against the glass – or brick wall – and listen. To some of Moore's ideas and ideals, to her unwavering judgement, but also to her unique, highly calibrated language, her grand, associative leaps, her wit and sarcasm, her cacophony of opinions and voices and sounds.

Everywhere I looked – in Moore's poems and letters, a Bishop biography, in the rooms of my house (a shell on the windowsill, a lizard skeleton on the mantle, a postcard of Cornell's *Grand Hotel Semiramis* pinned to the wall) there were references to the books and magazines she was reading, the literature and music and art that influenced her, the conversations she was having, the opulent interiors with objects she could never afford ('the peacocks, hand-forged gates, old Persian velvet – / Chinese carved glass, old Waterford, / lettered ladies'); the cherished gifts friends gave her (a nautilus, snake-fangs, a serpent star, anemones, a cricket-cage, a 'cocoa-nut' tied with a pink ribbon, a guidebook to Cornwall); the thoughts she might have been thinking, worried about, working her way through. As in a game of hide and seek, these are the kinds of details that zoom in before zooming, quickly – or not-so-quickly – out. Moore, as always, is in charge of the game. She's the one who's doing the hiding, and she hides well.

New Collected Poems gives us a chance to see multiple versions of 'Poetry', 'Propriety', 'The Steeple-Jack', 'The Frigate Pelican', 'The Paper Nautilus', 'Walking-Sticks and Paper-Weights and Water Marks', 'The Buffalo' and 'Nine Nectarines', merely a handful of the poems Moore notoriously revised and whittled away at over the years. The notes at the end of the book also include poems where the titles have changed from one publication to the next – 'To a Chameleon' was first published in *The Egoist* as 'You Are Like the Realistic Product of an Idealistic Search for Gold at the Foot of the Rainbow'. Early poems from 1915 to 1918 in the appendix, placed in a roundabout way after Poems 1963–1970, set the foundation for her later work, all of which give the reader a chance to catch glimpses of a less curated, less guarded Moore, one she took great pains, no doubt, to conceal.

And this was where I wanted more and less from *New Collected Poems*. *The Complete Poems*, a 1981 not-quite pink bismuth edition with the author's final revisions, which I found in the same used bookstore noted above, is a streamlined, easier, more focused read. In *New Collected*, I saw the potential to include more versions and variations of poems, to include more of the poems the reader doesn't usually get to see; delete the poems that no longer serve the poet or the time. At the same time, the notes section could have been tapered down, and the original index at the end of *Observations* (1924), which falls about a quarter of the way through, on pages eighty-one to eighty-nine of *New Collected Poems*, ultimately disrupts the flow of the book.

Or maybe it's time to challenge the approach of a collected altogether, shake up the linear order of the poems, add versions of the same poems beside one another rather than relegate them to the back pages.

This, perhaps, is easier said than done. There are untold versions of poems Moore wrote and other changes she made, not to mention the writing she simply didn't want the public to see. It was stipulated in her will, for instance, that her novel could never be published. As it was, her first book of poetry, *Poems*, was published in England, in 1921, by H. D. without Moore's permission.

In an interview with Donald Hall, Moore said, 'I think each time I write that it may be the last time; then I'm charmed by something and seem to have to say something. Everything I have written is a result of reading or of interest in people, I'm sure of that'. It seems as if Moore's restless mind was perpetually in a book, that it was the best, most reassuring place for her to be, that her encyclopedic interests were reflected in her poetry, and that her poetry was a way of recording what she saw, a way of writing through and against what she wanted to see.

As in the 'Anatomy of Man' section of the *Collier's Encyclopedia*, a series of transparencies can be peeled away to reveal different, more minute and intricate systems of the body underneath. With time and patience, a poem about a swan becomes a swan in a painting or a piece of porcelain – or perhaps the swan was always in the painting and suddenly becomes, with Moore's impeccable wording, 'real' – which then becomes a poem about beauty and patriarchy and ownership. A poem about fish wading 'through black jade' and a sun 'split like spun / glass' moves deeper, darker still, to an edifice that only appears to be dead.

I reread, fondly, the beautifully wrought sea in 'The Steeplejack', the meeting between Moore and Bishop outside the New York Public Library, the early poem 'Blake' ('I wonder if you feel as you look at us, / As if you were seeing yourself in a mirror at the end / Of a long corridor –'); I think about the subway tokens Moore and her mother insisted guests take at the end of a visit, the photographs of Moore looking most at ease beside a parakeet and elephant.

'Poetry is personal', Stevens said in a lecture Moore recorded in a letter. Moore wrote complex poems about love, institutions such as marriage, femininity, virtue, the treatment of people and animals and the world around her, all the while embedding found voices and quotes that are unattributed and stripped of context to shift power dynamics, derailing commonly held beliefs. All while constructing the calmest of facades, places where she could be Rat or Mr while Bear looked over her shoulder, where she could wear lovely blouses and hats adorned with flowers one moment, a cape and bowtie the next.

In 'Armor's Undermining Modesty', Moore writes, 'There is the tarnish; and there, the imperishable wish'. If lists are reminders, then *New Collected Poems* reminds us of a distinctly vivid and necessary voice, a Modernist who laughed with Alexander Calder and Martha Graham, threw the ball out at Yankee Stadium, dined with Cassius Clay (a.k.a. Muhammad Ali), and published her last book close to her eightieth birthday. Moore's poems are like armour, a lasting, much-needed protection, thick and tough and shiny, battered in places but ready for battle at any time.

Five Poems

PHILIP ARMSTRONG

In the Infinity Pool

The architects from the Las Vegas Sands
modelled their resort in Singapore
on three pairs of playing cards steepled like hands
and one more balanced on top.

On one side of the punt that floats
fifty-two floors above the city Raffles made
a brimming pool flows edgelessly into
the sweating upper airs.

Dry-haired guests line up, chest-deep,
elbows on the horizon,
holding their devices out on sticks

the way Hans Holbein might
have held his brush out squinting
as he stood before the King.

Headwind

A breeze that throws an arm around
your shoulder, armpit smell of pavement sun,

muscles high on their exertions, you could go
forever. That's just how it is right now.

Further on, cold-shouldered by the wind
you hitch your neck into a knot.

The wind picks up, it picks up sleet
and flings it in your face, which rosaceates;

gusts strong enough to blow the colour
from your hair, knock teeth out, ripple skin.

Hunched into the gale, hoar-frosted,
trembling, tetanised, you wonder

if you lay down now and closed your eyes
might they at least stop weeping?

Rising Sign

We're lying on the deck in sleeping bags, the night sky's clear
the water smooth enough that there's a gulf of stars above us
and another one below. Either the boat turns slowly round its anchor
or the sky does. My sister shows me how to trace the Pot,
which later I'll learn is the Hunter's belt, whose sword hangs
upward as he makes his astronaut's slow somersault.

My cousin is reciting every graphic scene from *Jaws*.
I'm too young to see the movie, but later as I turn
unsleeping in my bunk, hearing the water crackle
through the hull, darkness makes a screen
on which the same scenario plays time and time again:
the motionless night sea; me, floating naked;
far below, the pearl-eyed pale gigantic gaping fish
with wonderful celerity uprising and magnifying as it comes.

[Reprinted with permission from *Landfall* 227]

A Horizontal Light

You're following the track across
the eastern slope above the town, just
like you do most days. The sun's about
to drop below the north-west hills.
It shines a horizontal light upon

the grass bank at your side and casts
the life-sized shadows of a man with
an old dog. Next moment, from behind,
the shadow of a younger dog comes racing
through the others and away. And that's

the whole of it, right there, or else
as near as you can get to it, and gone
more swiftly than a man walks, dog runs,
sun sets, shadows follow over grass.

[Reprinted with permission from *Snorkel* 14]

Jeremiad

The morning easterly scrapes and scrapes
the torn-up estuary tide: whitecaps,
gulls and kite-surfers are scurf
blown sidelong.
                On Ferry Road the Prophet
Jeremiah waits to cross, his floral dress flaps round
feet black as bootsoles,
silver beard and ringlets stream back
from his leather face. Molten-muscled arms
push a stroller piled with plastic bags.
                      By the time
he gets there there'll be nothing left
but ruins: mud, sea-lettuce and the smell of ends
of drains. His lamentations.
                He trudges on
into the seething-pot of wind and sun.
His heart maketh a noise in him.

A Cricket for Pirandello

ANGELA LEIGHTON

for Roger Pearson

Nascere grilli è pure qualche cosa
— Pirandello

Our trade's translation, whether poems or prose –
      and here in Rome
struggling to render Pirandello's 'crickets'
I must lose the creature or else the dream,
meaning's gravity or else the grace.
Nascere grilli, he writes, to signify
fancies, daydreams, born on the hop...
but no insect makes a leap that's fit
for Englishing that device of wit.

So here's a leap-poem, Roger. It goes
      channel-hopping
from me to you, scrambling the frontiers –
since we who traffic from tongue to tongue,
mother to other, native to strange,
must make thought's impulse dance to the tune
that words call, by whims of their own:
idiom or pun, some self-stranging homonym,
the distant phones that ring in a phoneme.

Now skip: think ragwort, that hardy immigrant,
      taking root
in Oxford's first botanical garden,
later, on Isambard's cinder-tracks
riding westwards, seeding the dry ways –
but remembering still in the rails' sapped clinker
how once it rode the charcoal flows
of Etna's pyroclastic scree—
one hop ahead, gold-gracing earth's gravity.

So *Nascere grilli*... On a Sicilian plain
      small jumping jacks,
blue and orange in the hot afternoons,
would gleam beside his rockfast tomb –
flashes of insight, lost as seen.
We'll dream – so words go jumping free
from page to eye, from mouth to ear,
to hatch wild fancies in translation –
cricket-strangers on the ground's foundation.

Philip Roth

When Anne Frank Came to Stay

DAVID HERMAN

AFTER PHILIP ROTH DIED the tributes poured out. The consensus was overwhelming, both about what they said and, more interestingly what they didn't say.

They agreed that Roth was probably the greatest American writer of his generation. This wasn't always the case. During the 1970s there was some debate about whether he was in the same league as Bellow. Bellow had just won the Nobel Prize and in 1975 published his fourth great novel, *Humboldt's Gift*. Roth seemed adrift. The Seventies were not his best years. '1971, 1972, 1973, Roth – clearly something of a genius – pulled off three unqualified duds,' wrote Marin Amis. Twenty years later, however, critics began to ask whether Bellow was too formulaic, and worse still for a younger generation of readers, too cranky and right-wing. 'Who is the Tolstoy of the Zulus?' he asked in the 1990s, 'The Proust of the Papuans?' At that very moment Roth found an astonishing new voice. Four great novels in five years and the plaudits and awards flowed.

Think of those great set-pieces: the Chinese restaurant scene in *The Human Stain*, the high school reunion at the beginning of *American Pastoral*, Nixon's funeral in *I Married a Communist*. Those long, flowing sentences. The extraordinary images, the energy of his prose and the new elegiac tone.

Above all, Roth found his greatest subject. What was Roth's subject? The front page of *Libération* said simply: 'PHILIP ROTH: AMERICAN EROS.' Had anyone written about sex like Roth? But according to Dwight Garner in *The New York Times*, after sex, mortality was perhaps Roth's great subject. 'Old age isn't a battle,' Roth wrote in *Everyman* (2006). 'Old age is a massacre.'

Or perhaps it was the self? 'No modern writer,' wrote Martin Amis in the 1980s, 'perhaps no writer, has taken self-examination so far and so literally.' Elsewhere, Amis wrote that Roth's subject was 'himself, himself, himself.' Not just some abstract self, but suffering, raging, middle-aged, Jewish suburban man. Divorced, often childless, always in flight. Nathan Zuckerman fleeing from his 'entanglements'. 'Sabbath Absconditus'. 'His life was one long flight from what?'

One thing the tributes agreed on was that in the 1990s Roth found his true subject: America. Or, rather, a particular vision of America which caught the mood of the times. Born in 1933, he was formed by the New Deal and the idealism of the Second World War. Roth wrote eloquently about the America of FDR, the war and the GI Bill, the hard-working Jews of Newark and that great post-war moment caught by the scene of the high school reunion in *American Pastoral*. This, wrote Claudia Roth Pierpont, is what gave him 'the absolutely unambiguous sense he gained, during that war and because of that victory, "of belonging to the greatest nation on earth."'

Then came the Fall. No one has caught the mood of 'the indigenous American berserk' like Roth. 'America amok!' The trauma of Vietnam, broken families, political correctness gone mad, liberalism and decency under assault. And no one has written about what happened to American cities like Roth. Think of Alvin Pepler's rant at Nathan Zuckerman in *Zuckerman Unbound*, 'What do you know about Newark, Mama's Boy!... Newark is bankruptcy! Newark is ashes! Newark is rubble and filth!' At the end of the novel, Zuckerman visits Newark. 'The two-story apartment building where he had first lived was a ruin: The building's front door was also gone, torn from its hinges, and, to either side of the missing door, the large windows looking into the foyer had lost their glass and were boarded over... The building had become a slum.'

This is why the American flag is so important to Roth's 1990s novels. The rural post office that gets blown to pieces in *American Pastoral*, Sabbath wrapped in his brother's American flag. 'He took the flag down with him onto the beach. There he unfurled it, a flag with fortyeight stars, wrapped himself in it, and, in the most there, wept and wept.'

The tributes not only agreed that Roth's greatest subject was America. They also agreed about the Roth canon. The key works were *Goodbye, Columbus* and *Portnoy's Complaint* and then the American novels from *Sabbath's Theater* to *The Plot Against America*. However, there is something troubling about these tributes. They missed so much about Roth.

First, finding a subject and a voice was not easy for Roth. It is much more complicated and interesting than it seemed.

In 1961 Roth went to visit Bernard Malamud in Oregon. Roth was still in his twenties. He had just published his first book of stories, *Goodbye, Columbus*. Malamud was almost fifty. He was one of the most famous writers in America. He had recently published his masterpiece, *The Assistant* (1957) and one of the great post-war books of short stories, *The Magic Barrel* (1958).

This meeting was immortalized in one of Roth's greatest works, *The Ghost Writer* (1979). In this deceptively short work, a young writer, Nathan Zuckerman, visits E. I. Lonoff, a first-generation immigrant, who found a new voice for Jewish-American literature, a kind of Jewish-Russian-American writing, born out of the experience of the great immigration at the turn of the century. He had found a voice but, more important, he had a subject: 'life-hunger, life-bargains, and life-terror', a Jewish experience rooted in the traumas of east Europe and Russia.

There is a second writer in *The Ghost Writer,* Anne Frank. What is interesting about this appearance of Anne Frank is not the shock value, but what Roth does with her. Frank, of course, has a subject too, one of *the* subjects of the twentieth century.

This is the point. Zuckerman, like Roth, has missed the

great subjects of twentieth-century Jewish history. He was too young to have experienced the great tide of immigration and the old country. At the same time, born in safe America, he was spared the great traumas of mid-twentieth-century Europe. Throughout his career, Roth searches for a subject: from the Jewish suburbs of *Goodbye, Columbus* to Prague and Israel and then to America's post-war history, what critics called his American turn.

There is a third novelist in *The Ghost Writer*, Felix Abravanel, 'a 'writer who found irresistible all vital and dubious types, not excluding the swindlers of both sexes who trampled upon the large hearts of his optimistic, undone heroes [...]'. Abravanel, of course, is Bellow. Zuckerman heard him speak at Chicago, just as the young Roth had recently met Bellow in Chicago at a literature class.

It's clear what Malamud and Frank are doing in *The Ghost Writer*. But what's Bellow/Abravanel doing there? Bellow was hugely important to Roth. He was 'the "other" I have read from the beginning with the deepest pleasure and admiration,' Roth wrote in the dedication to *Reading Myself and Others* in 1975. They met in in 1957 and remained close friends till Bellow's death almost fifty years later.

Why did Malamud and Bellow matter so much to Roth? They were great writers, of course, the big names on the block when Roth was starting out. Roth was always more interested in literary father-figures than sons. He wrote more about Bellow and Malamud than Chabon and Foer. They did two things for Roth. First, crucially, they showed the younger Roth that you could write about the Jewish-American experience. They established it as a subject. Before *Augie March* and *The Assistant* who had taken Jewish-American life into the mainstream? *Augie March* was the first time a Jewish writer had won the National Book Award. It is hard to imagine today how highly Malamud was thought of in the 1950s.

Second, Bellow and Malamud represented two very different ways of breaking through. Roth wrote about Malamud's 'locutions, inversions, and diction of Jewish immigrant speech, a heap of broken verbal bones'. 'So little laughter', he wrote. Bellow was the opposite. As Roth wrote about *The Adventures of Augie March*:

> Bellow overthrows everything... In *Augie March*, a very grand assertive, freewheeling conception of both the novel and the world the novel represents breaks loose from all sorts of self-imposed strictures, [...] and, like the character of five Properties in *Augie March*, the writer is himself 'hipped on superabundance.'

'I didn't know what freedom was in a writer until I read that book,' Roth said. 'That you can do anything, that you can go anywhere.' Above all, Bellow brought together the high and low. He 'managed brilliantly', wrote Roth, 'to close the gap between Thomas Mann and Damon Runyon'.

This is the second point many of the tributes to Roth missed. He was a great writer, but he was also an outstanding reader and critic. He learned so much from Bellow and Malamud, of course, but more surprisingly from European and Israeli writers like Aharon Appelfeld and Primo Levi, Ivan Klima, Milan Kundera and Norman Manea. They gave Roth something very different. Roth

was one of the few American writers to immerse himself in 'The Writers from The Other Europe', the title of a Penguin series he edited in the 1970s and '80s, which introduced a generation to east European writers like Bruno Schulz and Milan Kundera. When Roth first met Appelfeld in 1984, *Badenheim 1939* and *The Age of Wonders* had only just been translated. Klima and Manea are not that well known to English-speaking readers even now. We so associate Roth with America that we forget how interested he was in writers from Bukovina and Czernowitz.

There is something else about this group. They can be divided into Holocaust writers and dissidents from behind the Iron Curtain. Like Anne Frank they had no trouble in finding a subject. In the opening sentence of Roth's interview with Klima, Roth writes, 'Born in Prague in 1931, Ivan Klima has undergone what Jan Kott calls a "European education."' Kundera (to whom *The Ghost Writer* was dedicated), Klima, Appelfeld and Manea were all born within a few years of Roth, but by the time Roth started high school in Newark, Appelfeld had lost his mother and grandmother, shot by the Nazis, and he had escaped from a ghetto and spent years hiding in the woods; Klima and Manea had been transported with their parents to concentration camps. Or, as Roth puts it in *Operation Shylock* (1993), where Appelfeld makes an appearance, 'hiding as a child from his murderers in the Ukrainian woods while I was still on a Newark playground playing fly-catcher's up'. That's what Roth means by a 'European education'. That's what drew him to these writers. Bellow and Malamud showed the younger writer that there was a Jewish American subject. The Europeans showed him there was another kind of Jewish subject and very different ways of writing about it.

When *The Plot Against America* (2004) was published nearly all the reviewers pointed out references to Sinclair Lewis and Jack London. Only one reviewer, Clive Sinclair in *The Independent*, pointed out the importance of two of these European writers to Roth's new book. In a fascinating interview with Primo Levi, Roth quotes the great Jewish Italian refugee historian, Armando Momigliano, who wrote, 'the Jews were less a part of Italian life than they thought they were'. Roth asked Levi, 'How much a part of Italian life do you think *you* are? Do you remain an impurity, "a grain of salt or mustard"?' Levi throws this back at Roth: 'don't you feel yourself, you, Philip Roth, "rooted" in your country and at the same time "a mustard grain"? In your books I perceive a sharp mustard flavour.' This, of course, is the question that runs through *The Plot Against America*. How much a part of American life are Roth and his Jewish family? Were they less a part of American life than they thought they were?

Then there is Appelfeld. Of course, Roth's novel about a right-wing coup owes a lot to Sinclair Lewis. But what about Appelfeld's *Badenheim 1939*, a great novel about how Jews are unsuspectingly overtaken by history, or as Roth puts in his interview with Appelfeld, 'the disorientation felt by people who were unaware that they were on the brink of a cataclysm', just like Roth's family in *Plot Against America*.

It is easy to forget, in other words, that the all-American Roth – author of a novel about baseball, others about Vietnam and Nixon – had carefully read and thought about his European Jewish contemporaries. Of course, his best work is full of references to Hawthorne, Melville and Sherwood Anderson but there's also another question: What if he had been born in Europe, not Newark, in 1933? When we think of *Portnoy's Complaint* (1969) we think of Roth and sex, especially *that* scene. What we don't think of is the scene between Portnoy and his older sister, Hannah, 'Do you know,' she asks, 'where you would be now if you had been born in Europe instead of America?' He doesn't have an answer, so she tells him: 'Dead. Gassed or shot, or incinerated, or butchered, or buried alive.' The key phrase here is 'if you had been born in Europe instead of America.'

Or what if some of the great European figures, Kafka and Anne Frank, had come to America? Roth plays with this idea. He was, of course, a playful writer, imagining alter egos and counterfactual histories. But what's interesting is the kind of counterfactual histories he imagines: European history coming to America. In the early part of his career he felt that American history was too small. Not interesting enough. When he returned to America at the end of the 1980s he had made a decision which changed his career: American history was plenty big enough, from the xenophobic Right in the 1930s and Korea and McCarthyism in the '50s to Nixon and Vietnam in the '60s and Clinton, race and Political Correctness at the end of the century. No more Kafka and Anne Frank. Now the references were to the American classics.

After their exchange about Momigliano and mustard, Levi went on, 'To possess two traditions, as happens to Jews but not only to Jews, is a richness – for writers but not only for writers.' Roth had a sense of several traditions: American, certainly, but also Jewish and European. This is why Roth keeps working away at the place of Jews in America. Take this extraordinary piece of *shtick* about Irving Berlin in *Operation Shylock* (1993):

> The radio was playing 'Easter Parade' and I thought, But this is Jewish genius on a par with the Ten Commandments. God gave Moses the Ten Commandments and then He gave to Irving Berlin 'Easter Parade' and 'White Christmas.' The two holidays that celebrate the divinity of Christ – the divinity that's the very heart of the Jewish rejection of Christianity – and what does Irving Berlin brilliantly do? He de-Christs them both! Easter he turns into a fashion show and Christmas into a holiday about snow. Gone is the gore and the murder of Christ – down with the crucifix and up with the bonnet! *He turns their religion into schlock.* But nicely! Nicely! So nicely the goyim don't even know what hit 'em. They love it. *Everybody* loves it. The Jews especially. Jews loathe Jesus. People always tell me Jesus is Jewish. I never believe them. It's like when people used to tell me Cary Grant was Jewish. Bull*shit*. Jews don't want to *hear* about Jesus. And can you blame them? So – Bing Crosby replaces Jesus as the beloved Son of God, and the Jews, the *Jews*, go around whistling about Easter! And is that so disgraceful a means of defusing the enmity of centuries? Is anyone really dishonored by this? If schlockified Christianity is Christianity cleansed of Jew hatred, then three cheers for schlock. If supplanting Jesus Christ with snow can enable my people to cozy up to Christmas, then let it snow, let it snow, let it snow!

Who else would play with the idea of a Jewish immigrant like Berlin writing the greatest songs ever written about Christmas ('White Christmas') and Easter ('Easter Parade')?

Jews are one of Roth's great subjects. They are everywhere. From his first book, *Goodbye, Columbus* (1959), 'Green lawns, white Jews,' as one of Roth's characters says some thirty years later, in *Operation Shylock*, to the antisemitism in *Indignation* (2008), fifty years later.

But it's not just that Roth's fiction is full of Jews – angry, crazy, masturbating, serious, funny. It's how much he does with his Jews. He was writing about the Holocaust ten years before Bellow. His story, 'Eli, The Fanatic' in *Goodbye, Columbus* is not only one of the great American short stories, it's also one of the great pieces of fiction about the Holocaust. Some of his Jewish families are safe and secure, enjoying that extraordinary moment of post-war American prosperity. 'The Jewish success story in its heyday, all new and thrilling and funny and fun.' But in *The Plot Against America* they are fleeing for their lives, victims of the American Right. Reviewing the novel in *The New York Review of Books*, J. M. Coetzee pinpoints the key questions at its heart, 'What is it to be a Jew in America? Does a Jew belong in America? Can America be his or her true home?'

Roth was once asked what is distinctive about Jewish writing. It's not the subject matter, he said. It is about a particular kind of sensibility: 'the nervousness, the excitability, the arguing, the dramatizing, the indignation, the obsessiveness, the touchinesss, the play-acting – above all the *talking*'. It's a funny answer and not untrue. What it misses out, though, is what he learned from Levi, Appelfeld and Manea. What Roth knew, and what the tributes don't really get, is the dark side of Jewish life in America, anti-Semitism, from Lindbergh in the 1930s to a small-town college at the time of the Korean War to Haldeman talking to Nixon in *Our Gang* (1971): 'There are a lot more anti-Semites than there are Jews, and the anti-Semites are with us generally and the Jews sure aren't.'

Roth did many things with Jews, but one thing he did, in particular, was to paint them into the American landscape. Take the small-town college in *Indignation* (2008). The college is in Winesburg, Ohio, the name of a book by Sherwood Anderson. Anderson's Winesburg doesn't have any Jews. Roth takes his Jewish narrator Marcus Messner there. It's not an *homage*. He's doing something else. He's imagining what happens if you put a Jew in Winesburg, just as in his great American novels he puts his great Jewish character, Nathan Zuckerman, in rural Connecticut. His fiction is full of American literary references and he seemed remarkably at home in all kinds of American places, from Newark and the Upper West Side to small-town New England. But he adds Jews.

This is, finally, what is most unsettling about all the recent tributes. They talk about how American he was. Of course, he was. He was invited to the White House to receive awards from two different presidents. He was one of the very few living American writers to see his work published in a multi-volume *Library of America* series.

But Roth's writing on America is more complicated than this suggests. Roth's is a very distinctive America. America plus Jews plus Europe. He kept thinking about what to do with his Jewishness as a writer and what to do with what he had learned from those European writers.

Many said that in the 1990s he found America as his subject. But finding a subject is too static. Roth's great books never rest. They are full of movement. At the end of *The Human Stain* (2000), the narrator says, 'I knew that my five years alone in my house here were over. I knew that if and when I finished the book, I was going to have to go elsewhere to live.'

Many of the tributes write about Roth as a monument. That's not right either. Not only was he too restless for a monument, he was too much of a mix. Much of his greatest work is about impurity and division. *The Human Stain* about a black man who passes for white. 'Eli the Fanatic' about an assimilated Jew in the suburbs who ends up dressed as a hassid. And, above all, Roth's America, which is never just one thing. Just when he has pinned it down as a version of pastoral, a maniac turns up with a bomb or a gun. Roth doesn't just move America centre-stage, he gives it a history, and, crucially, a history which is *catastrophic*.

Many of these tributes say more about British culture than about Roth. Our fascination with America. Our lack of interest in east Europe and Jews. Our fantasy that writers don't read other writers. Our interest in Philip Roth as one of the great writers of our time, but not in why he wanted to write about what happens when some Holocaust survivors arrive in an assimilated American suburb or when Anne Frank comes to stay.

Five Poems

CLARE JONES

Living fossil

There were days I doubted I'd ever spoken words.
      I saw clawed toads all without tongues.
There was only smoke where the fire was,
      so I sat in whale light. I slept alone.
I found each morning rocks that rose
      like shoulderblades out of the sea:
      a life was a long time
      to be no one's father, being
         a shovel in the ground.

When stardust flecked the river stones,
      and leaves like greaseprints smudged the paths,
I looked for signs left behind by birds:
      seeds eaten, broken grass, a line across the lily.
I looked for feathers rubbed off like scales.
      My inner ear staggered at the climb.
      I knew no wind
      would make it through so much:
      it would seem I knew much then
         of what I'd never know.

What raids have reapportioned
      all those stars and streamlights?
I know some ways do not wear out,
      but surely some ways do.
Shouts pass through stone yet still things move,
      though enough is not enough and can never be.
It appears: there is the way, which is an old, old word,
      and there are winds that turn it over:
      the dust brushed back,
      the grooves pulled through,
         and teeth fused to the jaw.

Barkdust

It is a fact that you were
in a shaft of sunlight
somewhere. Sunlight
full of dust, and that dust
once another: it wasn't just
your skin. But some of it,
it was. No one makes that up,
that once it made up you. These
things do not seem true. But
they are true enough. Cinnamon.
Quinine. Bark pulled roughly
from trees until it tears. Rolled
like scrolls and ground, surrounded,
packed in glass that's shaken, sold.
The light inside you, gold. It is
and was the gold dust. Young men,
old men, they searched for it
in streams. They called it panic.
It was in their blood. It was a ribbon
going nowhere, slowly. It was true,
true enough. It was in your skin
once. In a shaft of sunlight somewhere.

If there is some mistake

A stub of a strawberry with a little leaf-ruff won't root
or sprout but it grows all the same. Look. Even a foot
from the bulk of the compost heap
it sends out this delicate fungus. It hurries. It loots.

It spits. It sits under a makeshift tent of spider
webs. It learns how to ask for one minute longer.
From whom exactly? The heat. The dark.
That is what sent the fungus, anyway, and then the spiders.

In school, there is a poster of a food web and spiders are at the top.
The strawberry is in the book about fruit. It is not
in the food web, and even if it was, it would be beneath the spider.
That's how it is in the real world. It's not something you can stop.

Pretend? Sure, you can. But you shouldn't. Don't pretend the strawberry's glowing,
the grey hair around it is kind of beautiful in the moonshine, the right lighting,
the spiders are gone, and pirates are all exaggerated stereotypes,
and the dark is not hot and continuous but cold and final and no one's right.

Oilbird

It seems you were a dolphin. In a former life.
So, given that, what is it that you do?
Go live in a cave? Eat only laurel fruit?
I say you should take care. Take care of this life.

This life, it will not last. It will not last for long.
When birds grow up, they turn. Flesh turns into air.
And if the world is dark, then it makes more sense.
No, air doesn't last. Never, not for long.

As long as you disappear, all the torches spread.
An uncanny feeling surely fills the cave.
A din like crickets fills. It fills the nesting space.
And a light that looks like water, water up ahead.

Error

I will make a chain. I will make a chain react.
I will put it in the desert where there are vultures and there are rabbits.
I will not tell anyone about it except in passing and they won't get it.
I will come each day to the same line
　　　but with different errors.

I will find water in the desert with my knees just so, tucked under.
I will dig a hole that, no matter what, will not fill in completely.
I will build a nest inside of it that I'll come back to later.
I will come each day to the same line
　　　but with different errors.

I will mark the time. I will mark the place and number.
I will look into the hole I dug the way a watchdog ought to.
I will forget where I dug the hole first, but in the end, I doubt it matters.
It will come to me with the same line
　　　each day with different errors.

Four Poems

VONA GROARKE

As If Anything Could

A paper from the year before last is the start of
my tonight fire. Where was I? What have I done?
It's not as if the world was shouting, 'Do this!' or
'Do this!' at me. And it's not as if learning one thing
means unlearning one thing else. Home is to lie
when you need to lie, a bowl of tomorrow left
by the bed and a window at the height of your hand
to open, like a diary, so the days and all their equipage
slip lightly, oh so lightly, from the room.

Against Boredom

I marshal the kind of questions
answered by car parks, part songs and stained glass.
How you get from one to the next
is like chainmail
or sunlight on chainmail,
irrefutable.

Like that time when, for something to do,
I unhooked a screed of cloud
laid it out over my bed,
let my hands imagine sea creatures
and new continents, a philosopher with a beard.

Whimsy? Perhaps. Or metaphor.
You choose,
I'm afraid I can't help you with that.

I am busy observing an evening scramble
over tall buildings, even mine,
through car parks and parked cars,
one blue eye fixed on loose talk
one brown eye on the dark.

See how close I get?
And all without scarcely moving
except for my hands replacing,
minutely, a screed of cloud
on a backdrop of blue
that is anything but,

we all know that

but what else is there
for it to be?

The House with No Clocks

The days are long and leisured
but the years, the years
pass by like the dark swoop of the stingray
as it slides under the jetty
— Sarah Broom, 'The Years'*

Sea at the front, wind at the back,
the run of the house with the grapefruit tree
has been given to me. Mine for five days
this stack of wood, this patchwork quilt,
the keys with the dolphin keyring,
all this giddy rain.

Mine to sleep on a borrowed bed,
to measure my nights by the measure
of what another life has been
as though one could line up moon
and stars, tally them by fireglow,
breathe in light years between.

Mine to know what to do next,
how to make good on days that close
as darkness closes when a car
drives through. Mine the bare bones
of a quiet hour, then the skitter of words
tipped by the wind when a roof leans into it.

Mine to reckon an equals sign
with my own black pen.
Mine the space to either side,
mine the pivot, mine the promise,
mine the stumble, mine the sway,
mine, thousands of time.

* from *Tigers at Awhitu* (Carcanet, 2010)

What I Didn't Know Then About the World

I had a yellow dress that summer
but the mountain, in its so many greens,
put it about that I was not what I seemed,
said in its feathery, wind-flipped way:
only one of us needs to be naked here
and I don't see why it should be me.

'intricate accommodation'

on Dick Davis's *Love in Another Language: Collected Poems and Selected Translations* (Carcanet) £20

A.E. STALLINGS

DICK DAVIS's *Love in Another Language: Collected Poems and Selected Translations* represents over forty years of original poetry and translations from the Persian. Davis is hard to place in some ways, like an accent that has softened over time, travel and distance. Born in Portsmouth, Davis has spent almost all of his adult life out of the United Kingdom, living for a time in Italy and Greece, residing for eight years in Iran (1970 to 1978, in the lead-up to the violent Revolution), where he met and married his wife, Afkham (to whom this volume is dedicated), and finally settling down in Columbus, Ohio. He is probably better known in some American poetry circles (associated, in particular, with the poets sometimes described as 'New Formalists') than in British ones, and better known in academia as a Persian scholar than as a poet. What makes him hard to pigeon-hole, however, is also what makes him distinctive. As the *Collected* brings home, here we have a poet who is not only technically skilled and widely and deeply read, but a worldly poet engaged in history and politics, whose most timeless qualities end up being the most topical. Likewise, Davis is among a number of contemporary verse translators who are challenging the notion of translation as in some way a secondary art dependent on an original rather than a primal generative act in itself. (Translation is, I would assert and I think Davis would agree, a kind of linguistic sexual reproduction.) The inclusion of a 'selected translations' with the 'collected poems' goes some way to making that case. In a world in which human migration and displacement will only increase and intensify, a poet who crosses borders of language and culture, and is attuned to the rhyming ironies of history and current events, is, however accomplished and polished in traditional English verse technique, a poet who belongs to these unsettled and unsettling times.

In Davis's brief, modest 'prefatory note', he explains that 'like most habitual writers of poetry who live past middle age, I tend to prefer my more recent poems to the earlier ones – readers of course often disagree with poets' assessment of their own work [...]'. The note is itself very telling – that use of the word 'habitual', for instance, which implies poetry not as a turn of the spirit but a way of life, artist as craftsman, a poet made, rather than born, and made by making, over and over, day in, day out. I find I agree with him: I too prefer the more recent poems, though it is also fascinating to track the arcs of subjects and themes, and to watch as Davis 'enters the clarity' he loves.

His 1982 'Letter to Omar' comes roughly a third into the book, but is, in other ways, central. Written in the Rubaiyat quatrains introduced into the English language by Edward FitzGerald's famed translation of Omar Khayyam (and further naturalised by Swinburne and Robert Frost), the verse letter to Omar Khayyam is equally indebted to W.H. Auden ('Letter to Lord Byron') and to Byron himself, the tripping triple rhymes being more Byronic than Audenesque ('imperilled / FitzGerald / herald'; 'dollars / scholars / Ayatollahs'; and maybe most emblematically, 'traitor / creator / translator'). Discursive as suits the epistolary, the poem, in speaking to the dead, explains the poet's own journey into translation and poetry, while also, as it were, serving as a letter of introduction from Omar Khayyam to his pioneering translator, Edward FitzGerald, another literary hero to Davis. My description sounds tortured and difficult, but the poem is itself sparkling and playful. 'Merely slick' sets us up for the closing rhyme (and the letter's close), 'Sincerely, Dick'.

Certain images and tropes, concerns and themes, can be traced through the book. Chess is a rarefied but not unpopular subject with poets (Ezra Pound, T.S. Eliot and Cavafy all have chess in their poems – as do Omar Khayyam and Princess Jahan Khatum for that matter), and Davis has at least three chess poems, 'A Short History of Chess', which begins with its Indian origins and ends with an epigrammatic, 'It took the West to twist the tale / to strategies of faith and sex'. A second poem that features the game is titled 'Exiles', and Davis sets up a tension between two men battling for a black-and-white victory or defeat on the chessboard, though of course for an exile there are only gradations of loss, while their wives gossip about actual (deposed?) royalty and lost fortunes. In both of these poems, the poet is himself absent from the scene, though he is the witty intelligence in one, and perhaps witness in the other. A third chess poem from a later book (*Touchwood*) seems to contain the earlier poems while expanding on them. This poem has the irony of the other two, with an added historic sweep; but by inserting himself into the poem, the poet achieves a note of *ubi-sunt* melancholy and a surprising personal conclusion. Set against a backdrop of ruined grandeur and fallen empires (the Ozymandias effect, perhaps), the simple, storytelling past tense, ballad meter, the plain diction, the neutral register ('adolescents') provide the unruffled surface so that you come upon its emotional depths with the suddenness of unexpected tears. I'll quote it in its entirety:

A SASANIAN PALACE

The great hall at Firuzabad
    Lies open to the weather –
I saw two adolescents there
    Playing chess together.

There was no splendour to distract them;
    Only a cavernous shade
Cast by the drab and crumbling vault
    Where silently they played.

So much of Persian verse laments
    The transience of things
And triteness was mere truth as they
    Pursued each others' kings

Where kings had given orders for
    Armies to march on Rome,
And where I watched their game awhile
    At home, and far from home.

One of the striking effects of the *Collected Poems* is how a metaphor in one poem can rub off onto another one in which it is not, technically, present at all. A poem that makes no reference to chess at the same time brings that image to mind. The later sonnet 'In the Restaurant', discusses yet another of Davis's exiles, 'A Queen in exile, she presides at table' – now she is a 'plump matriarch' – but once in her youth she had 'risked her life / To cross Beirut's bomb-cratered no man's land, / Defying anguished parents, to say "Yes" / and be an unbeliever's outcast wife'. Somehow the mention of a queen who can cross a checkered no man's land in a single, game-changing move brings to mind for a moment the chessboard of earlier poems.

In 'Farewell to the Mentors', Davis nods in the direction of four poets who are avowed influences – Fitz., Edgar, Wystan and Housman (that is, Edward FitzGerald, Edgar Bowers and Auden) – 'Old bachelors to whom I've turned / For comfort in my life' – only to realise in the area of marriage and teenaged children they have nothing to say to him. Another influence whose presence I felt often in reading through the *Collected*, one which is I think less conscious, is Philip Larkin. Davis does not have Larkin's bleak misanthropic bitterness, but they do sometimes share a tone (that of 'Home is so sad'), a certain flat melancholy that comes out in some of the poems about childhood, especially when unrhymed, and certain cadences. There is something Larkinesque at the end of 'New Developments': 'As if their earnest play could substitute / Forever for worlds crueller and less cute', or in a line like, 'The heart has its abandoned mines'. Reading 'No Going Back', a poem about how the poet's mother preferred the deep, tragedy-inflected voices of Robeson while the speaker prefers 'high sexless voices', 'transcendent, bright, no weight, no tears', I am put in mind of several Larkin poems at once, but in some ways it is almost a response, reversed in the mirror, of 'Mother, Summer, I'.

Poems that are allusive rather than elusive, nimbly metrical, fully rhymed, stanzaic, proportioned, syntactically clear – *measured* in every sense – might seem to some readers on the surface dated. In fact, only a few of the earliest poems in this collection have a sepia-tone, a late mid-century mannerism. 'A Mycenean Brooch' (with an epigraph by Yvor Winters) or 'The Youth of Telemachus' (which ends 'all night he views the changing sea') are perhaps much as one might imagine from the titles, accomplished, unsurprising. (I hope I have latitude to say this as a writer who might well have committed the same titles!) But Davis becomes more and more particularly himself, perhaps through the act of translation. As he points out, creator and translator rhyme. He is as influenced by medieval Persian poetry as by any English master or Western classic (and makes use of Persian verse

forms, monorhyme and ghazal and rubi'a), and doesn't shy from alluding to poems, poets and characters most of his readers are unlikely to know. Names of composers and painters, of arcane writers and books, of far-flung places, a flash of German, an etymology, the plot of an opera, have not the sense of an elitist's dropping of names, or an academic bristling with footnotes, but something of the opposite: a cherishing of civilisation and its humane productions by someone who has experienced tragedy at first and second hand, on the historical and personal level.

As the poems face up, more and more frankly, or more and more overtly, perhaps, to biographical sorrows and trauma (the suggestion of an abusive childhood, dysfunction, secrets, a brother's suicide), and the vicissitudes of the people and places of Davis's sojourns, including Iran and its revolution, to which he lost friends and acquaintances, the poems clarify and resonate. Even the story of how he met his wife in Tehran in 1971, suggestions of which flicker through various poems in various books, suddenly comes into sharp focus – he simply tells us the tale in the recent poem 'The Introduction', which begins with a bit of a *recusatio*: 'Autobiography's not something I / Have felt in any way impelled to try'... and ends on the inevitable English rhyme, here also absolutely earned: 'When I came round at last the doctor said, / "We very nearly gave you up for dead; / This nurse, Ms. Darbandi here, saved your life." / This was my introduction to my wife.'

Davis is, in fact, a love poet of the rarest type – one who principally writes love poems for his wife. These poems braid throughout the volume (his first book appeared in 1975, after his marriage), and we seem to watch as that love matures, complicated with exile, in-laws, children and age. Davis has two early-ish poems that refer to Ausonius's 'Uxor vivamus' ('Wife, Let us Live...'), itself a response or perhaps a rebuttal to Catullus 5. One is titled 'Uxor Vivamus', and the other ('To His Wife') is a graceful translation. Poems about marriage, and epithalamia written for the weddings of others, appear throughout. 'Marriages as a Problem of Universals', 'Memories of Cochin (an Epithalamion)' 'Hearing a Balkan Dance in England' (in which a bride appears). Even among the subset of love poems to wives, erotic verses are rare. In Dick Davis's 'Monorhyme for the Shower' (in, with sly appropriateness, two symmetrical and shapely stanzas), the poet hymns a glimpse of his wife's breasts: 'The movement of that buoyant pair / Is like a spell to make me swear / Twenty odd years have turned to air.'

Despite the melancholy and pain that emerge in poems about childhood particularly, and the different flavour of melancholy, the nostalgia that comes with a lifetime in a sort of exile and among exiles, Davis resists despair, choosing love and praise. In 'A Monorhyme for Miscegenation' (yet another epithalamion), we realise that marriage and translation aren't just subjects to which Davis returns, again and again, they are metaphors for one another:

Mixed marriages, it's true, can make
Two lives a dire disaster zone.

But only half since when they work

(As my luck, and my friends', has shown)

Their intricate accommodations
Make them impossible to clone.

What is translation if not 'intricate accommodation' as meaning in one language must be embodied in the words of another? And what is marriage if not learning 'Love in another language'? Davis sums up his biography and *ars poetica* in the candidly titled 'A Personal Sonnet', which recapitulates the facts about his dead brother, his 'gadding years' in Greece and Italy, etc., but which concludes:

The presences I've loved, and poetry –
Faces I cannot parse or paraphrase
Whose mystery is all that they reveal;
The Persian poets who laid hands on me
And whispered that all poetry is praise:
These are the dreams that turned out to be real.

Davis's worldly wit and irony never become sour, only bittersweet, precisely because ultimately Davis turns to praise, for the flawed world, for complicated relationships with children, for the 'intricate accommodation' of marriage, the compromises and surprises of translation, and for poetry and language itself, perhaps the only true home exile can carry across borders. That the book ends on a selection of Davis's Persian translations seems appropriate, and indeed seamless. Thus the poems are in the roughly chronological order, composed in the 20th and twenty-first century, largely in Columbus, Ohio, but the book ends smack in the fourteenth century, in Shiraz. The last poem in the volume is one Davis translates by Princess Jahan Malek Khatun. And indeed Davis seems to be speaking through her, as well as vice versa, when he concludes the *Collected* with this valedictory quatrain (ruba'i):

The roses have all gone; 'Goodbye,' we say; we must;
And I shall leave the busy world one day; I must.
My little room, my books, my love, my sips of wine –
All that is dear to me – they'll pass away. They must.

She lived through another Iranian revolution, in 1353, when all the men in her family were slain by a conquering warlord. As Davis says, 'Most of her poems are love poems, but a few comment on the political struggles she lived through'. The same, *mutatis mutandis*, of course applies to her translator as well.

Two Poems

Sophie Hannah

A Man with Straight White Teeth

Today, at an appointment with my dentist,
he revealed his own teeth. That's right – he opened
his mouth, flared his lips and flashed a full set.
If you ask him why (and don't bother, please)
he'll say it was part of a demonstration
of how to brush, and how not to brush,
for my benefit and for no other reason at all.

He would never admit to resentment, or wanting to hurt me.
He had teeth all along, of course, and I should have guessed,
though he kept them well hidden. I should have jumped up and pressed
his top lip hard with my index and middle fingers, to check.

I made it clear what I wanted and hoped for. That's why he lied.
When a dentist utters the words 'my teeth', it ought to mean
his patients' teeth, not his. Where, otherwise, is his sense
of ownership? What's at stake in my mouth for a man
with straight white teeth of his own?

All of this ought to go without saying. No one would take their car
to be serviced by a mechanic who owned a car himself
that he kept tucked away in a centrally heated garage.
Imagine asking a man to paint your house, then being told
that he owns and lives in a house that's more 'his' than your house is.
'Ever heard the phrase "conflict of interests"?' I asked my dentist.
He gave me a look that suggested he'd rather I kept my mouth shut,
and yet he's a dentist and I am his patient, and that
I told him, right there? That's the whole problem.

The Only Copy on Earth

Satisfied that my flawless characters have behaved
impeccably for three hundred and fourteen pages, I type
'The End' and glow inside. They are nothing like anyone I've known.
Not once does the heroine lose her cool, smack her head
with the heel of her hand at the crassness of minor characters
who in any case are not crass like real human beings.

Having done this many times, I know what's expected of me
next: I'm to put my three hundred and fourteen pages out
to be read by people who cheat on their spouses, drive
with their mobile phones in their hands, muffle their chakras with sugary
drinks, bellow at their tiny, quaking children, pray
to sputtering gods who are all about rules, and all
for two hundred and fifty grand a year. That's no longer enough.

I can't bear to put my pristine characters through it.
'Please,' they say, 'Not again. Everybody these days is so
detestable. How can we make it through page after page
if we don't sympathise with at least one reader? There's no one for us,
the super-rational and the wholly good, to care a damn about.
They're all ruthless narcissists, stubble-heads and the most inert of bores.'

So tomorrow my team will arrive: little carpenters and their pet
engineers. They will make me a wooden box frame with metal hinges –
a frame that's opaque, a box that won't open without breaking.
All I'll need then is a taste-maker with a gallery – white, central, chic –
on the prowl for his next protégé, who'll be someone you couldn't invent
if you tried for a million years.

Not a sliced up shark this time, not a tent full of antique sex
but a book you can't see and can't read. You can only know
that it's excellent and it's there, though you'll want to doubt both if you care
how you look, how you sound; if you want your money's worth.

If the taste-maker plays his part, I'll play mine,
make us rich every March on the dot. I'll do all that I can
to ensure that the terrible people miss out. Shall we say
seven hundred grand for the only copy on earth?
I will love what I do so much if it can be this.

From the Archive

Issue 143, January–February 2002

MIMI KHALVATI

From a contribution of ten poems
entitled 'The Inwardness of Ele-
phants'. Fellow contributors to this
issue include Grevel Lindop, Michael
Hamburger, Jane Yeh, Christopher
Middleton and John Gallas.

MAHOUT

We trust each our own elephant
till our own elephant kills us.
The attendants holding the silk umbrellas,

the one who plies the fan
of peacock feathers, the man
with the flyswatter of yaktails.

You cannot cheat on the amount of oil
poured in the lamps for an elephant
will always honour the pace of the ritual. [...]

Four Poems

THOMAS ROSENLOCHER

Translated from the German by Ken Cockburn

BORN IN DRESDEN in 1947, Rosenlöcher lived in the German Democratic Republic until reunification in 1990. He first completed a commercial training before studying at the Johannes R. Becher Literature Institute in Leipzig. He has been working as a freelance author since 1983 and is a member of the Saxon Academy of Arts. He lives near Dresden.

Rosenlöcher published two books of poems in the GDR before *Die verkauften Pflastersteine: Dresdener Tagebuch* (*Sold Cobblestones: Dresden Diary*), 1990, gained him readers in the West. Poems from his 2001 collection *Am Wegrand stand Apollo* (*Apollo Stands at the Wayside*), translated by Tessa Ransford, appeared in *The Nightingale Question* (Shearsman, 2004), and he undertook a short reading tour in Scotland in 2005. His recent books include two collections of poems, *Das Flockenkarussel* (*The Snowflake Carousel*, 2007) and *Hirngefunkel* (*Mindspark*, 2012).

My Wooden Tongue
('Das Holz der Rede')

I'll be right there. I quickly headed down
the mazy pathway that went snaking through
the dying garden, sneaking off from itself,
where in the early light the apple tree
was standing where, indeed, it always had,
but somehow squint, and looking black as death,
and then as I approached it, just hang on,
slowly lowered itself toward the lawn
and laid its trunk upon my shoulder, so
I almost buckled underneath its weight,
saying to myself: such is life.
One man drives a car he takes for granted,
another supports a tree,
while in the next-door garden
screeches an apocalyptic saw.
Yet someone here has still to do the work
and be content. That is my part.
It's better, as of now, to be upright
than buried flat out underneath the trunk,
I thought in my upstanding way,
as falling rain soaked through my trouser legs
until the sunshine made me steam with thanks,
before you called again at supper-time,
and darkness settled calmly on my shoulders.
The tree supported me as I held it,
and held me up as I supported it,
until one morning on my nape I sensed
a ticklish nest of tips and filaments.
The plant was greening yet. And I, betwittered,
surrounded by a cloud of little buds
which, white, were sending out a reddish haze,
felt myself wobbling underneath my load
so that – again your light inside the house
was shimmering this way, and your long wait
increased a hundredfold among the twigs –
among the snow of blossom fading out
to black beneath the stars of colder snow –
I carried on my back the whole of space
and was about to fall asleep, yet with
my wooden tongue rasped: yes, I'll be right there.

Reading Horace ('Die Horazlektüre')

Can you think back to the winter again,
when up there the wood's edge froze to a tumult
of rigid verticals glinting with frost? –
I asked, from the foldaway chair, reading Horace.
But you simply laughed – in the middle of summer?
And really the fields had already risen
high over the countryside's measuring rod.
And though the sun had long disappeared –
there seemed to be fires abroad in the wood –
still you were busy with hoses and watering-cans.
When even the children – 'it's home-time!' – 'Nooo,
we're playing hide-and-seek!' in the scattering light
'one two three...' went quiet – 'found you!' –
and a final, beer-fuelled cry of despair
rose from the next village and drowned in the fields,
the swing kept squeaking and squeaking and drew out
ode after ode. And finally even
the old man who hadn't been seen out for months
hobbled expressly up to the fence:
'I ken nou,' he called, 'why there's nae shut-eye!'
And lifted his stick to shoot at the last
golden gleam in the sky, bang bang.
Can you think back to the winter again,
when the white wall loosened itself from the woods,
surrounded our house for days on end,
and the snow-drifts kept rising, right to the window?
I said, from the foldaway chair, lost in weeds,
but instead of an answer all I received
was a white stream of frothy watering-water.
And the odes of Horace grew dark and became
illegible cohorts of marching ants.
And the willow below, each leaf of which
had turned in on itself, a motionless night.
Against day-blue sky. Rustling. A star.
'Presumably Venus,' I elaborated.
'All right, come on then.' 'What, now?' 'Why not?'
It's possible, surely, to think of the winter.
It's possible, surely, the feet of one
pummel with fists the rear of another.
It's possible, surely, we freeze.

Stopover ('Die Einkehr')

One afternoon, as the yard was finally
filling up with children and sparrows, as those bearing briefcases
made their way home to prepare supper,
there was a whirring in the air
and two men with wings set their feet upon the earth.
Everyone stood stock still. But old Mr Lot
straight away came down in the lift,
greeted the men respectfully, went to the shop for wine
and other residents brought steaming saucepans,
sat with them at table, ate and saw each other
in a new light. And then came evening.
And look, the men's wings
shone with the painters' colours
as though a new ocean had appeared,
its scent the keys of heaven. When they had eaten,
the angels arose, thanked and blessed all who were there,
for never before on earth had they seen gathered together
so many of the just. Presently certain gentlemen arrived
and their caps were iridescent in the last stray gleam
as they identified themselves and asked the strangers to accompany them.
Everyone stood stock still. But old Mr Lot
berated God,
who yet again had sent his angels
down to earth too soon
and now, as though nothing had happened,
was spreading manure on the fields of heaven.

Could happen to you
('Passiert dir auch noch')

From right behind Orpheus, Endler appears.
– Sod summer, he says, no fags and no booze.
I promised her though, since I almost crossed
the River Jordan – water on the lungs.
Could happen to you. On the other side,
by the by, was Müller, drinking cheap Scotch.
Instead of offering me some, he called,
'have you put your affairs in order yet?'
At that I thought I'd better row back.
She though was weeping: no fags and no booze,
sod summer! – With angry-ironic steps
Endler walks past the roses towards
the lever-arch file which has been expecting him.

ACKNOWLEDGEMENTS
'Das Holz der Rede', 'Die Einkehr', 'Die Horazlektüre' from: Thomas
Rosenlöcher, *Das Flockenkarussell* © Insel Verlag Frankfurt am Main
und Leipzig 2007. 'Passiert Dir auch noch' from: Thomas Rosenlöcher,
Am Wegrand steht Apollo © Insel Verlag Frankfurt am Main und Leipzig
2001. All rights reserved by Suhrkamp Verlag Berlin.

Truth, My Child...

BEDILU WAKJIRA

translated from the Ethopian Amharic by Hiwot Tadesse and Chris Beckett

is not something you inherit, like a lump sum
or a language, faith; it doesn't
populate the busy places, in the bustle

or the chatter, that's not truth talking,
no! this little box of human bones,
God's likeness, that's where truth sits,

where something in you whirrs and sings
as you peer into your depths
and dance along, whoop, weep, open your big eyes.

Mind, a row of shining teeth is not a smile,
not everyone who sheds a tear
is crying. Remember, child, the truth is shy.

We sparked a life in you, your Mum and I,
but each of us has our own heart,
our drum-beat drowns yours out or pinches it to ours.

Our only wish is to defend you like a flower
from the wind, from any evil day.
We think of Jesus in the deserts, temples, rivers,

teaching truths he found inside himself,
so we hang the loose string of our jumbled lives
around your neck and wish you well.

Don't call me 'baba', child, and question me.
I am a house of private and external truths
like bricks that jostle in the walls. But still I stand.

If they call my truths a lie, I call lies truth!
Don't be like me, I sometimes break
into a laugh and hide behind the sound of it.

Don't count on politicians, either: their words are sweet
on radio and TV screens, but deep inside they stab
their brothers, rattle in their liars' parliament.

Listen, yes, do listen, child, no-one dies from listening.
War cries, edicts and disdain all hurt, but trust
is tricky, too, you have to think beyond the clutter in your ears,

past the accepted truths that people read
and make their faith, like that to which
a generation of Ethiopians pledged allegiance in the 80s

and ended up its prey, its roadkill, flesh-filth, blood-scum.
Truth is not always just, child,
sometimes it is illness, cruelty, emaciation...

take Emperor Tewodros, towering at Meqdela,
refusing to back down, even when Britain
came with guns and elephants, did his truth survive?

take Belay Zeleqe who drove the Italians
out of Gojjam, they had to hang him
as a common thief to put his fire out!

Archbishop Petros, who some say *wrecked his see,*
met a hail of bullets trying to keep
his life and work and faith on the same page...

how many men and women choked by ropes of truth
around their necks, left families
to lift their bodies down and count the cost?

It was not lost on them that if Belay Zeleqe
had bent his knee and licked a boot,
if Petros preached even a whisper of the Fascist creed,

they would have been dressed in gold,
enthroned precisely for dethroning truth!
But they knew lickspittle brassy fanfares rot:

the only truths that do not crumble are imprinted
in a country's heart, how people live, not just
the words they utter but everything they do not say –

enter their homes, child, lie on their sprung
or hay-stuffed mattresses, eat mouthfuls of their kitfo,
take a handful from the ashuq, sink yourself

into the muddle of their daily lives, this little shack
where our humanity has roots
and grows until it is so strong it will redeem

whatever mischief time can throw at it:
take your own time, child,
find your own truth and live with it.

Every Wrong Direction

Dan Burt

CAMBRIDGE EXPOSES FOOLS in the nicest of places. Stupidity is denuded among the world's best tended, charming, romantic lawns, river banks and studies. An understated question, diffident comment, private word pointing out misquote or wrong fact, a comment ignored, subject changed, unmasks fraud and presumption in the most delicate manner, the ensuing nakedness all the less bearable for the tact, delicacy and discretion with which pomp, cant and pretence are exposed. Sometimes it wasn't until hours after being fatally skewered that I flushed, realising how dumb I'd been. A Cambridge college is a bad venue for parading in the emperor's new clothes.

Completed in 1831, St John's neo-gothic New Court is laid out in the classic 'E' pattern of an Elizabethan manor house. Hugh Sykes-Davies (HSD), St John's Director of English Studies, had rooms in New Court's Stairwell I, on the first floor of the E's north-west wing. His set overlooked the Cam and Backs to the south, west and north through large mullioned windows, and was a college jewel. Beyond its oriel window seat, April through October, undergraduates and tourists punted sunward in the late afternoon, under the Bridge of Sighs, past Clare Bridge, King's College Chapel, and on to Grantchester, while undergraduates, a lucky few with girlfriends in those pre-coed days, played croquet, lazed on the Back, or read in the Scholars' Garden. December through March the westering winter sunlight, bent almost horizontal by the declined winter sun, kindled Hugh's study, and the Wren Library across the Cam, as red-kneed choir boys in shorts and crimson lined cloaks scurried to Evensong on the lager-coloured gravel path below. Chez Hugh, the clock on Grantchester church still stood *at ten to three*, and there was *honey still for tea*.

I knocked on Hugh's door for my first supervision at the beginning of my second full week at college. *Come in*, came a tenor command. Inside, a short, pot-bellied, impish looking fifty-five-year-old, and two gowned second year undergraduates, sat waiting at a large table in the study.

Hugh had assigned 'symbolism in modern British poetry' for my debut essay, a topic with which I was familiar. I'd dipped into Symons, sampled Baudelaire, Rimbaud, Mallarmé in *en face* editions; read Yeats, Eliot, bits of Pound; knew what the *Yellow Book* was, and European history from 1875 through the Great War, before I sailed for England. I beavered away for a week, refreshed my recollection of the style and times, read commentators, poets and by my essay's Friday due date produced a fifteen-page paper.

Hugh had it front of him as I sat down. He welcomed me, introduced the two students invited, I later realised, to show me how supervisions were done, then picked up my essay. *Interesting Burt, very interesting.* I'd hoped for more, but was too callow to appreciate how damning *very interesting* was. *Now let me see... Tell me, what exactly is a 'symbol'?*

Through all my reading, labour, thousands of words too many, it was the unconsidered question. For a second time in eight days my bowels loosened. It was, of course, the right question, the foundational interrogatory, and we both knew, Hugh and I, that it was new to me. I had read all the books, but not thought critically about what I'd read. I hadn't learned to ask foundational questions at college in America. Working-class American Catholic colleges are not known for critical or subversive thinking, and at mine, LaSalle, I was consumed with cramming what I should have learned in secondary school, as well as the college coursework. Some say Cambridge's only purpose is to teach you to ask two questions: *What does it mean?* and *How do you know?* The lesson had begun.

*

HSD was a Surrealist, poet, novelist and English Literature scholar, as well as much-married, Marxist eccentric and member of the thirties' *God that Failed* generation. He came up to John's in the mid-twenties, earned a starred first with viva in the then new English Tripos, and was appointed a university lecturer and Fellow of the College. There he remained till his death, Johnian to the marrow.

His circle included famous intellectuals, critics, writers, artists and spies: Wittgenstein, Russell, Keynes; T. S. Eliot among the older, Thom Gunn among the young British poets; Burgess and MacLean among the spies. A Wordsworthian, fisherman and devotee of Isaac Walton, he wore a black pin-striped suit, tie and waistcoat unbuttoned at the bottom to allow his pronounced pot belly to accommodate dining, the ensemble flecked with ash from the mottled meerschaum calabash he drew on ceaselessly, lit or cold.

The son of a welsh clergyman, he lugged his Marxist hod with him from Wales's green coal valleys. No place in England was more hospitable than thirties Cambridge to all shades of red, especially to young academic highflyers. Hugh shared a flat with Guy Burgess, one of the Cambridge 5, and Roy Pascal at The Lodge, on Chesterton Lane, known as the 'Red House' in deference to its residents' politics. Hugh was long rumoured to be 'the fifth man' of the thirties Cambridge Russian spy ring, until Anthony Blunt was unmasked in the sixties.

The Apostles, founded in 1820, is the premier Cambridge intellectual society. It has twelve current members, all undergraduates, their identities secret. When an Apostle *goes down* (graduates), those still *up* choose a new member from among the brightest university undergraduates. Hugh had been an Apostle, as were, for example, before and after him, Tennyson, G. E. Moore, Russell, Rupert Brook, E. M. Forster, Wittgenstein, Keynes, Jonathan Miller and Amartya Sen.

Anecdotes about him were rife. He wed his first wife, the poet Kathleen Raine, when he was twenty-two, and divorced her shortly thereafter. He's said to have borrowed a bike within minutes of finding her making love to someone else and pedalled sixty miles to London to file the divorce papers. One of his four wives he married twice, the second time so she'd receive his pension when he died.

An inveterate showman, he announced at the start of a lecture he gave on psychotropic drugs and literature that he'd just taken mescal to prime himself for it. For a poetry reading he tape-recorded what he was to read while accompanying himself on the accordion, hid the recorder beneath the lectern before the reading began, and halfway through laid the accordion aside, closed his mouth and started the recorder with a hidden button. The audience was gob-smacked – instrument laid by, reader mum, words and music continuing. A don who heard him that night forty years ago talks about it still.

Hugh's pedagogy contained a strong iconoclastic streak. He surprised, unsettled, upset and provoked you to examine the common, as well as the exotic and sophisticated. *I try to do something different every day*, he said once, *even if it's walking a different way to the Sidgwick Site* (lecture halls).

His supervisions were like conversations with a favourite, slightly Socratic uncle I never had. He didn't preach or lecture, and, all but once, gave no *ex-cathedra* advice. He questioned, observed, told anecdotes. A supervision on moral seriousness in art, and its pretensions, he pointed by telling an anecdote about a famous French literary scholar attending a Proust conference at Cambridge. Hugh invited him to Hall, and after dinner they toured the college library. The Frenchman was bored. Hugh asked if he wished to see the college cellars, and hearing *Certainment!*, down they went to the caves. The Gaul appraised the stock and, engaged at last, enthused *Quelle jolie bibliotheque vous avez ici!* [What a delightful library you've got!].

T. S. Eliot wrote the religious pageant *Choruses from The Rock* soon after the Second World War to raise funds for the preservation and rebuilding of bombed-out London churches. During a supervision on the place of Eliot's later poetry in his *oeuvre*, Hugh mentioned he'd gone with Eliot to the *Choruses* premier, during which Eliot leaned over and whispered, *You know, Hugh, I'm not sure I believe some of this stuff myself.*

Hugh never visited the US. His left-wing, anti-war politics did not sit well with America's anti-Communism and sanctimonious imperialism, especially as the Vietnam war ramped up. One day he explained the root of his distaste succinctly, and tactfully, given my then nationality, by likening America to a brontosaurus, whose thoughtless sweep of its tail destroys half a forest without realising what it's done. Nevertheless, he enjoyed American poets like Dickenson, Frost and Bishop, and it was he who kindled my love of Lowell and Ransom.

*

As Director of English Studies, HSD chose eight to ten students each year to read at John's for the English Tripos. Among them he included a *wild card* (his term), an applicant to whom the customary entrance requirements would have denied a place but whom, for whatever reason, Hugh thought worth a try. I was his 1964 *wild card*.

I didn't know when I entered John's if I would have to study two years or three for a degree. Graduates of affiliated universities, such as Harvard, Yale, Columbia, Princeton and Stanford, could do it in two. LaSalle College in Philadelphia was not among them. I took ship understanding John's would watch me for a term, then recommend to the university whether to allow me to take my degree in two years.

In the third-class lounge of the S. S. *Rotterdam*, one day out of New York bound for Southampton in mid-September, 1964, were three superior young American males. They had come top of their undergraduate class at Columbia a few months earlier, their reward a two-year Kellet Scholarship to Oxbridge to study for an Honours BA. One was deep in a chess match with an elderly *Mittel-European*; the other two watching. The chess player was Richard Epstein, a tall, gawky New Yorker going up to Oxford, the two others to Cambridge. They were the first quondam Ivy-League undergraduates I'd met.

The Cambridge-bound Kellets and I fell into conversation. When I complimented their comrade's play, they said of the three he was the star, best at whatever he did. Epstein won the match, rose, spoke briefly in German with his opponent, then turned to where we were standing. *Boy, you looked pretty good*, I said, extending my hand. *I could have been a grand master, but it wasn't worth my time*, he replied, and strode off, no introduction, no handshake. I met a number like him a few years later at Yale Law School.

I entered Hugh's set for my second term's first supervision on a cold, sunny January afternoon in 1965. *Come in Burt, come in. Sit down. I have some news for you. The university considered the matter, and I'm happy to tell you that last week the University Senate awarded LaSalle affiliated status; you can take your degree in two years.* So now there were six affiliated institutions – Harvard, Yale, Columbia, Princeton, Stanford and LaSalle College.

Hugh leaned forward, removed the bowl from his calabash, knocked doddle into an ashtray, paused:

Dan, I may call you Dan, mayn't I?
Yes.
You work very hard, don't you?
Yes.
Well, you know, you didn't come here to learn anything. You came to get an education. Why don't you take it a bit easy?... Do you like cinema?

No one before had said work less, or distinguished learning from education. Until then, life had one end: win; only the object differed: fight, drag-race, girl, degree, law school, money. I'd read Jaeger at LaSalle, at least struggled through it, but paideia remained a faint, distant Siren. Now, there was a chance to remove the wax, and attend her song. I did, was beguiled, and succumbed to three passions: for art, in almost all forms; *custom and ceremony*, Yeats' rubric; and sailing. They are passions still.

*

Kettle's Yard was a living work of art in 1964. Jim Ede, a Tate curator in the twenties and thirties who championed

Nicholson, Brancusi, Wallis and more, moved to Cambridge in 1956. There, he melded three tumble-down, ancient cottages across the street from John's, known as Kettle's Yard, into one, painted the walls white, left the blonde oak floors bare, filled it with the simplest furniture, stones and sea glass gathered on St Ives' seashore, and his collection of modern art, and lived there for thirteen years. Tuesdays, Wednesday and Thursdays he opened it to students, and I visited often, as did many others, including Nick Serota, progenitor of Tate Modern. Kettle's Yard was a house with art in it where an elderly couple lived, when I dallied there, not a museum. From it I took my idea of what a living space should be.

Once a week or more, I spent mid-afternoon there, staring at paintings and sculptures, talking to Jim, and day-dreaming in a small white room under the eaves in the north-west corner of the house, the only furniture a day bed opposite a west-facing window. On a supporting wall that bifurcated the entrance to that room hung a large Nicholson, precise rectangles, arcs, circles in dun brown, grey and white straining for sublimity; on the floor across from the day bed a small bronze Gaudier-Brzeska bird swallowed a fish; on the bed itself a striped, rough wool Connemara throw. Either side of the winter solstice the sun slipped almost horizontally through the window, swamped the day bed and wall behind, and made the space, for an hour or two, a rare warm place in winter Cambridge. I sat mesmerised on the day-bed, watching dust motes jig in the sunbeams, while the dying light drew a shadow over Brzeka's hungry bird. It was my first experience of *calm, luxe et volupté*; in my brown studies those spastic motes still dance.

Alfred Wallis was an unschooled, retired harbour pilot in the early thirties, living alone in a one-room cottage in St Ives. Poor, bereft after his wife died, to pass the time he began painting ships in harbours and at sea, the world he knew, with left-over boat paint on cardboard. The vitality and presence of his paintings, found in the very best 'Naifs', are unique for their threatening, cold, ice-grey seas and silver spindrift tops, so real you'd turn up your collar while you gazed at them. Ben Nicholson stumbled upon him in the early thirties, painting outside his cottage, and brought him to Jim Ede's attention. Nicholson and others gave Wallis brushes, paint and boards on which to put it; Jim brought the works to London to sell, and bought many himself; his Wallis collection is unparalleled.

A closet at Kettle's Yard was crammed with paintings there was no room to display. You could borrow one at the beginning of term, on the promise to return it at term's end. All came back, intact. Each term a Wallis hung by my desk. One hangs in my London library today, purchased from Christie's half a century later.

*

Henri Gaudier-Brzeska would have become France's greatest modern sculptor had he survived the First World War, and the small oeuvre he left behind impeded recognition. Jim owned a trove of his works, championed him, and wrote his biography *Savage Messiah*. In December 1964, Jim was advising Paris' Musée d'Art Moderne on a forthcoming major Gaudier-Brzeska exhibition, to include a replica of his atelier. But he had not seen the exhibition space, and old age made travel a trial. (There was no 'Chunnel' then.) When he learned I was about to spend two weeks in Paris trying to improve my French, Jim asked if I would visit the space in the museum proposed for the exhibition and give him my impressions to supplement the floor plans he'd been sent. I agreed, and he wrote a note introducing me and my mission and told me to present it to the Directeur Général of the Louvre when I reached Paris.

On a raw December morning, wide-eyed, awed and deferential, I entered the Louvre's administrative offices. It was my first time in France, first visit to an art museum anywhere. I handed Jim's letter to an official and was escorted immediately down long, dim, high-ceilinged sixteenth-century corridors into the Directeur Général's grand suite. He greeted me warmly as *un ami de Monsieur Ede*, said a few words in French I couldn't understand, then pulled a slip of headed paper from his drawer, scrawled a few words, put it in an envelope, and told me to present it at the Moderne's ticket desk. Outside I opened it and read, in French simple enough for even me to understand:

Madame, Monsieur
Laissez passer M. Dan Burt, a tous les musées de France.
    [s] Directeur Général, Louvre

A free pass to every museum in France.

Mornings in Paris, I'd walk from my *pension* down the right bank of the Seine to the Moderne, present my pass, and wander there for an hour or two. After a few mornings the guard recognised me and waived me through. A massive reclining bronze Maillol nude at the entrance stays with me, as do the Legers, and, above all, the sense of being an initiate, not visitor, loose in a great store of art.

Forty-five years later I sat in the Directeur Général's office again; only the Directeur had changed. This time the gift was in my power – Cy Twombly's planned painting of the Salle de Bronze's ceiling, which I was negotiating, in English, on behalf of the benefactor paying for it.

Two Poems

GREGORY O'BRIEN

Mihi

for Margaret Hickey, 1927–2018

The birds and animals of our mother's land greet
   the birds and animals of your land.
Her waterways, tributaries
and flooded plains
   greet yours. Now she is gone, she joins
the dead of her tribe
in greeting
    your dead. And her dead
birds and animals offer this, their heartfelt
address, to your dead birds, animals.

And to the living. Her constellations greet your
   constellations and if these happen to be
   the same constellations
they wrap their arms around
   themselves.
Her fruit trees, in season, greet
   your fruit trees,
     their fallen fruit.

Our mother's clouds and insects
   fly to embrace your clouds
and insects. Her architecture, roads,
bridges and infrastructure
   rush to greet yours.
Her molecules on their upward trajectory
entwine with yours, the colour of her eyes,
hair and skin. Her language,

with its past
participles, figures of speech,
   the sounds and tremors
which are its flesh and bones,
these words go out
to greet your words and
   to greet you –
these words
which will never leave her.

Conversation with a mid-Canterbury braided river

'Fifteen apparitions have I seen; / The worst a coat upon a coat-hanger' — W. B. Yeats, 'The Apparitions'

Moved, as I am
immovable, like you

I turn over, I sleep
on my side

nestled in the
watery fact

of you. I fall about, collect
my thoughts –

another thing we have
in common – I get ahead

of myself, I meander
so as not to

lose my way. I rock
and sway.

I digress. And this is how
I come back to you

bedded and besotted, body strewn
with inverted clouds

migratory birds, dawn-lit
improbable.

Like you, I have
my sources; I wade

the long waters
of myself. My ear

to the ground or
the constant applause

of your rapids. You are your own
concert, open-air, a solitary leaf

crowd-surfing downstream
and the occasional beer can thrown

from a passing car. Lately there has been
talk of you as

lapsed or recovering, dispersed
drained, interrupted or

resumed. And this
my sleepless night, my apparition:

an insect walking this land –
a coat-hanger on which might hang

a bright green shirt, a stream led down
a long avenue of hosepipe and

aluminium, a river flowing
sideways, its taniwha

reduced to a drizzle or fine mist
a trickle from

an automated tap. Your position on this too
is inarguable

as if argument was ever
a river's way.

Braided, you tell me, I was
upbraided, scrambled across

siphoned and run ragged by hydrotrader, flood
harvester, water bottler, irrigator

and resource manager. This riverbed is
my marae, the long legs of wading birds

my acupuncture, these waters
my only therapy.

On clear nights
galaxies enter me, planetary bodies

like swimmers. How many minds
a river has – caddis and mayfly

eyeless eel and
native trout. As an argument

this might not hold water
but neither does

a paddock gone around
in circles

or a skeletal arm endlessly
scrawling its initials in

a sodden green ledger. Whichever way
the river doesn't flow

I remain undecided, as is
water's way.

I disperse, lost for words
I dry up.

I saw an apparition, an insect
walking this riverless land

earthbound stars
rattling, beyond reflection

along a dry
river's bed.

Four Poems

MATTHEW SWEENEY

The Exit

At first it seemed perfect: the green sea,
and a silver pony bounding towards me, as if he
was waiting to carry me anywhere in the world.
He bit me, though, took an apple chunk out of my arm,
where the blood spurted. I should have run away,
but where would I go? The road I'd escaped on
stopped dead, leaving a field where nothing grew
except marram grass. And I saw sheep eyeing me,
while baring their teeth, and crows circling in the sky.
And suddenly, out of some concealed loudspeaker,
came cackling laughter, loud enough to be heard
on the island, where they'd captured me five days
before, when I was playing chess with myself on
the tiny pier, a glass of beer warming on the wall.
I sat on the ground, covering my eyes and my ears
in turn. In the lull before the next attack (which
would come) I asked myself why I was surprised.
This was surely inevitable, and just what I deserved –
what had I tried to do to stop the teenage suicides,
for example, or girls blocked from getting abortions?
I waited for the crows and the sheep, and worse
surprises, but nothing came. The laughter stopped,
so I opened my eyes. A gate had appeared
two hundred metres away – it was black and tall,
with sculptures of owls on it, and it looked open.
I got to my feet, looking round me. I knew this could
be another trap, and where I ended up could be
worse again but I let my instinct lead me there.

Crocodile

He was in the river, as if he belonged there,
dawdling in the water with two eyes above it –
twin periscopes that flicked from one bank
to the other. I mean, this wasn't the Zambezi,
but the River Lee! I stopped to stare at him,
and that drew his famished attention to me.
Time to vamoose, I reckoned, hurrying across
the Shakey Bridge, at the end of which I turned
just in time to see him climb onto the bank
and start to wriggle up the steps. Jessie Owen's
run in the Berlin Olympics, 1936, was my model
as I crossed the road and hared past the pub
to my gate, which I firmly rammed shut, then,
after entering, slammed the door of the house.
I positioned myself at the front downstairs
window, half-camouflaged by the curtains,
sipping my glass of water, and sure enough,
two minutes later, Mr Crocodile nudged the gate
open with his snout, and let his little legs
bring him halfway up the path where he lay himself
down to wait. His tail wagged slightly like a dog's.
Was that a smile when he bared his teeth,
or was he simply showing me what daggers
they were? How on earth could I withstand him?

The Angel

I look out the window a lot, while reclining
on the bed. Oh, I turn away when it's raining
but today has been fine. I was watching the birds
flying over the university when I noticed a very
large bird among them, swooping and rising
on the thermals till it changed tack and headed
my way. In fact it came to the house next door
and perched on the chimney. Well, I say perched
but stood would be more accurate, for it wasn't
a bird, it was actually an angel, yet it didn't
look like any angel in a Renaissance painting.
No this fellow came straight from 1950s Britain –
the dark tapered suit, the black suede creepers,
and the hair swept back in a quiff. He was
staring at me – with difficulty, I realised, when
he reached back and took from a haversack
a spyglass which helped him have a good look.
After he was sated he reached back again to
release a grey kestrel which he loosed in my
direction and I watched it come straight as
an arrow to bounce off the windowpane
with a sound like a thunderclap. Poor bird,
I thought, then I said bad, incompetent angel!
Was that supposed to be a message for me?
At that, the teddyboy took off and glided over
to smile, then veer away – even the wings
seemed suede, and were grey. I lay back
to make sense of it all, but couldn't, so I
traipsed downstairs to check if the kestrel
was dead, or had been there in the first place.

The Chess Match

I got a phone call to tell me the chess match
was this afternoon, in Fitzgerald's Park.
What chess match?, I asked. Come on, you're
representing your county, the voice said.
My county was at the other end of the island
and I couldn't represent a rock at chess.
And besides there was no big chess set any-
where in the park. I'd seen one in Freiburg
when I was a student – I used to sit and watch
intellectual men wage chess war over hours,
struggling to manoeuver the giant pieces from one
square to another, while onlookers cheered.
I admit it made chess a spectator sport
but that was in Germany, *Mittel Europa*,
not a modern Irish city, and I hadn't played
chess in decades. Even so, to my surprise,
I pulled on my black coat and dodo-skin hat
and crossed the Shakey Bridge to the park.
I'd got myself into the mood for a contest.
I thought about asking two young women if
they'd be my supporters, but they wafted by.
Maybe there'd be bus loads of loud people
wearing green and yellow Donegal scarves.
If there was, I missed them, the big chess
set too. I queued for a coffee in the hippy café
as the police car pulled up, siren blazing.
There was a bomb, we were told, we needed
to scarper. So this was yet another trap, I
realised, as I bounced along the riverbank,
like a baboon given a head-start by hunters.

Five poems from 'Ring Cairns'

PETER RILEY

We are incredible. Our tombs say so. We are
the children of work-destroyed bodies. We walk
up to the circular cemetery at midnight

and shout: '*Lazare, veni foram*' *I know you're in there!*
Come out of it. And tell us the truth,
after the event, do we wake up or what?

And if we do, what does the world matter? No,
he says, and the owls signal along the woods each
to each in heraldic hoots: Brother, sister, it turns out

there is no knowing, as we've always known.
They say no more but, credible creatures, defy
the regression of polity, crunch a few mice and amen.

*

I remember... I forget what I remember.
Ah, Robyn, gentle Robyn, your soft locks
on my forehead and nobody said a word.

It's not a folk song. It's a technicality.
Six Canada geese in formation way above
Brighouse station, brilliant arrowhead finding its home.

On the riverside lawn where our parts agree
we sip Cuban cocktails served by black boys
in white jackets who know better than anyone

that you cannot force an ending on the bright air of ever
with nothing resolved into justice. For we are many
and will not forget. We are the them that doesn't.

*

Press the cork back into the neck
and the day is concluded. Tomorrow,
Messiaen in Blackburn Cathedral and total crisis.

Total, inescapable, end, crisis. And why not?
Why after 300 years not? The gentle harmony
at the Labour Club confirms our sweet failure,

the crashing tones, the squeaking mice,
the unstoppable reproduction, *Gloria*
in excelsis and peace on earth, they all know

it's not happening. The dawn song
closes the festival as first light touches
the tips of the forest and the dancers go home.

The tired musicians case their viols knowing
that in the long night of their absence there
has been such violence. Twist the cork out and pour

another half glass no more, raise it to those who died
while we parodied. The gate in the long wall
is open, the nymphs are banging on the door,

the dead turn in their hotel beds knowing that for all
their work and hopes love lies cloven.
And not whosoever and not things happen

but specifically, by design, to create the enemies
needed as targets for the malice upon which all
their empire stands, and all their courts combine.

They have capped our hearts and closed our sight on
blinding detail, which gets us out of their way. We had best
march quietly on in thought, cap in hand.

There is a pavane that is the music of that march.
It rolls many times over. It presses against the lungs.
It speaks quietly to the nearest person, 'Sandwiches and

beer when we get to Pontefract. We have not finished yet.'
'Thanks, joy be to you, and nourish your patience, we have
some way to go yet.' 'We shall never forgive them for this.'

*

Goodbye, then, white dove. Goodbye clear, *luce*
serene clear *e chiare*, light, true speech, goodbye.
And yet the ground over yonder is rich with simplicity.

First sunshine cast along the canal represents
eight Canada geese as a golden flotilla.
Under their gold they worry and watch as usual.

What kills me in love is when
the world falls into the song and
laughs itself out again.

Sé que me muero, me muero de amor.
The gentle, best-meaning, synapse lights its lamp.
And did those scarred and blistered feet.

*

I'll stop that now. I'll stop dying of love and,
so trimly dight with feathers like a lady bright
I'll sit alone, singing by night, in foreign tongue

Te whit, te whoo, te whit te whit te whoo. Are not
the final words of the *Agnus Dei* a desperate plea,
that we not be made to awaken from death?

We beg in the end this one favour, bought
with our only distinction, save us from this savagery
to be roused into a light not of this earth

and spoken to! what could be worse? To be
forced back into language. *Dona nobis pacem.*
Te whit, te whoo, te whit te whit te whoo.

Sweet Yorkshire owl, come join the chorus
echoing the London wolves, and together we'll sing
a dirge for dying souls. Souls. Souls. Souls. Souls.

Poetry of the Spanish Minorities

Six Basque Poets (ed. Mari Jose Olaziregi; trans. Amaia Gabantxo) Arc Publications
Six Catalan Poets (ed. Pere Ballart; trans. Anna Crowe) Arc Publications
Six Galician Poets (ed. Manuela Palacios; trans. Keith Payne) Arc Publications

MARK PRENDERGAST

DOES GALICIAN LITERATURE DIFFER from Basque literature, Catalan literature? What space does the poet write from in a postmodern, globalised world? These bilingual anthologies of Spain's minority language poets cannot provide the grounds for a definitive answer to these questions, but they do give the English reader a place to start. What about the reader? Is buying one of these volumes online a bit like deciding which take-away cuisine to log on and order for tonight's dinner? If English reading culture is hybridising, does this in any way affect greater sovereignty for minorities? In the context of Basque literature, L. Elena Delgado has been critical of the extent to which edition and translation operate as means of constructing palatable cultural identities for 'universal' consumption. Delgado questions the extent to which minority literatures are read as supplements to the dominant literature, drawing a comparison with the role of the Grand Tour in finishing off the education of the wealthy westerner, and arguing that: 'This brief period of exposure to carefully chosen "local" cultures and sites, only served to reinforce deeply ingrained ideas about the universality and historical continuity of supposedly homogenous Western European culture'. Not surprisingly, in her introduction to each of these volumes, series editor Alexandra Buchler has a more benign take on reading in translation. She argues for translation as a three-way dialogue between poet, translator and reader and makes the interesting observation that translation is integral to the practice of the poets of minority literatures: 'Writing without having read poetry from other cultures would be unthinkable for the poets in the anthologies of this new series, many of whom are also accomplished translators, for, as well as considering poetry in translation part of their own literary background, they also regard it as an important source of inspiration'. Reading minority language literature deconstructs the formative exclusions of national literatures. Delgado goes on to argue for an ethics of reading in translation with, 'The willingness to accept that some texts, and some realities, refuse familiarity and simultaneous translation, and therefore our perception of them might always be somewhat blurry. Ironically, it is with this humble acknowledgement that we begin to engage with what has hitherto remained out of (our) sight'. As Spain's modern history demonstrates, exclusionary nationalist literature aligns itself with absolutism, while a literary culture that generates translation, and that associates in translation, may be more democratic.

After the last Spanish election resulted in another hung parliament, the Basque Nationalist Party (PNV), in a very Basque way of doing business, became kingmakers, passing Prime Minister Mariano Rajoy's 2017 budget in return for some new-fangled pork (high speed trains) and, more significantly, increased financial autonomy. In her introduction Mari Jose Olaziregi outlines the history of suppression of the Basque language under Franco, when the language could not be spoken in the street, through the cultural activism of Basque writers in the 1960s, to the current legislative framework that recognises Basque as an official language of Spain. Yet, Basque's status is perennially fraught in that it is a minority and an isolate language, that is, unrelated to all other living languages. Joseba Sarrionandia has lived out this era, being imprisoned for his involvement with the armed separatist group Euskadi Ta Askatasuna (ETA) (who finally formally disarmed in April last year) before escaping into permanent exile. In his poems, Sarrionandia, a meta-literary and intertextual poet, interrogates what exile means. 'A Runaway's Luggage' articulates the fragile non-identity of exile: 'We have learnt new grammar rules, but fingers still point: / "He is not from here"'. In one her letters Simone Weil discussed exile, in what she understood as its very Greek and very Catholic dimensions: 'this place of the soul's exile is precisely its fatherland, if only it knew how to recognize it'. In 'The Minotaur Speaks' Sarrionandia reaches the same conclusion, refashioning the myth using diction that is down to earth, not elevated, in a setting that is not palatial but homey. The poet and the Minotaur share a couple of beers, lamenting not valuing what they once had and losing what they now hold dear, the Minotaur's final words a simple paradox: '"We live in exile, wherever that is"' (91). Miren Agur Meabe's poetry expresses a more sanguinary response to the pull of impossible desires across fluid boundaries. Somewhat unfortunately for the only woman represented in the anthology, her poem 'Brief Notes (1)' brings the faraway closer through the figure of the female at the ironing board. Like many poems with similar aims, it works at once to generate both empathy (faced with mediated images of trauma the speaker spontaneously lactates) and dissociation (the child in the image is identified only as 'black'). Sympathy towards the other, without complicity in their plight, is the take out message. But, while the generation of correct feeling is an important start, it is insufficient as an end in itself. In 'Water Dreams (III)', Meabe plays with the image of the bed as a body of water and the desiring body's fluidity. 'Aeolia (III)' also addresses the metamorphosing body. In a turn found in some of Meabe's other poems, the voice of the poem travels back from the land of the imagination bereft but clear-sighted: 'I am not Aeolia nor am I wandering. / You are not nourished by my pulse, / these are not the waters you navigate'. Like Meabe, Kirmen Uribe's poetic of lively humanism holds to the conceit that embodied truths are all that is left when language fails. 'The River' sketches the deep emotions submerged under communal and individual lives, captured in the image of a poplar in the town square torn down by the wind: 'Its roots an upturned hand / that wants to be touched'. In a longer narrative poem ('Mahmud'), Uribe conjoins Spain's Islamic heritage and the contemporary migrant experience. However, in skipping over Spain's imperial past, despite his best intentions, Uribe risks reinforcing Spain's identity with the invaded, not the invader. Uribe's poem 'The Visit' sits with familial anguish, its wounded, powerful reprise sounding an authentic note: 'I don't want promises, I don't want remorse, / just show me love'.

Catalonia's separatist sentiment was tested again in last October's referendum, which asked whether the autonomous community should move to full independence as a republic. In his introduction, Pere Balart argues that the recognition of achievement of Catalan literature has lagged behind other cultural fields. His survey of Catalan poetry to the present day is useful; his anthology as a sampler of current poetic practice, perhaps, less so. As with Olaziregi, Ballart finds space for just one female poet and, reading Ballart's praise of Gemma Gorga in his introduction gives the impression that she might have almost been chosen for her attributes as a writer who reinforces gender stereotypes. For Ballart, emotion in Gorga is expressed through 'recourse to childish and domestic symbols' and 'modest everyday things', her introspective poems 'always expressed in a serene and immutably placid tone of voice'. Certainly, this is so in 'The Aged Penelope Speaks' where the figure of the shrewd negotiator out to salvage what she can of her domain is reduced to a disgruntled homemaker, cum self-funded retiree: 'This emptiness from so many years lived / in the man's shadow. / An I, absent from myself'. Does a sample of two constitute a pattern? 'A Woman' is another selection where the emblematic figure is standing at the ironing board, a domestic deity working while the household sleeps, a tireless figure whose work is never done: 'Behind the steam of centuries, a woman / is ironing, making the most of the last of the light'. While these poems do express unease, and, in their original context would read differently, here, surrounded on all sides by men, one can't help but read them as, in some sense, the female poet being kept in her place. Ballart describes Manuel Forcano as Catalonia's foremost contemporary love poet, whose Cavafyesque evocations of the Middle East are sites of contact across civilisations. In his introduction, Ballart betrays his own defensiveness towards the charge of exoticism in Forcano's poetry, arguing that: 'These subjects attract him, not because they are exotic or decorative, but because they allow him to unite the autobiographical element of his poetry with a meditation on ethnic and cultural otherness'. 'Law Governing Aliens' explores desire without horizons, the disingenuous voice of the poem positing this as less a quest for enriching experience, more subjecting oneself to the charity of others: 'I eat what there is, / what they give me. // Until, / law in hand, / they expel me / or I go out to search for new horizons. / Invisible hands push us. // I don't know whether I prosper. / I survive'. The long episodic poem 'At the Café Sahel in Aleppo', exemplifies what Ballart refers to as Forcano's ability to shape out of a poem: 'a dazzling register of instants of plenitude' (19).

However, in an anthology published just as the Syrian Civil War erupted, the poem jars in its aestheticising of war and inequality. The voice of the poem compares the lovers to a destroyed city, describes their affair as a kind of fleeting victory. Revisiting Aleppo today, what would this victory look like? But this is not likely, the poem trailing off into fading memories: 'I remember you as the blind men / who in the courtyard of the mosque / recite for a gift of alms / the surah of light from the Koran. / I give them a coin / that is not worth the brightness they no longer see / nor in me / your absence'. Josep Lluis Aguilo's poetry conflates the classical and the popular, referencing Raymond Llull and spaghetti westerns, drawing arresting correspondences in sometime Borgesian fantasies. 'Words', gives space to the poet's little dictator, that megalomaniacal drive to experience the flow of clarity: 'when everything combined in a single term / and one word was synonymous with the universe'. 'The Contract' contrasts past glories and a compromised, domesticated present: 'Every horseshoe is a semicircular contract / that we renew regularly and which says: with blows we love you, we always have need of you, / behave well'.

Manuela Palacios, likewise, provides a history of Galician poetry, cataloguing a range of writers not included in her selection for interested readers to follow up. Her genealogy culminates with the generation of poets, first published in the 1990s, whose work, she argues, expressed a confident autonomous Galician poetic, the outcome of being educated in the language throughout their schooling. Some of the poets in Palacios' selection grapple with the civic implications of the lyric in a minority language culture, their work pushing beyond the boundaries of identity. Yolanda Castano's work explores the figure of the female poet, its masks and illusions, in a variety of tones of voice. Some of her titles are in English, the poems addressing the difficulties of expression when English is your second, or third, language. In 'Less is More' the powerlessness of being blindsided by love lost is underlined by the title and captured in the refrain: 'He didn't say'. And the limits of language are always of the body for Castano, as are its triumphs: 'those distant words / you're never going to read, / they're orbital because they're mine, this here / is mine, mine, like this my tongue. / Mine' ('The Winner Takes All. The Muse Goes Home Broke'). Xose Maria Alvarez Caccamo's father was a leading figure in mid-twentieth-century Galician literature and, in 2008, was honoured in the annual Galician Day of Letters. Big boots to fill. In the same year, Alvarez Caccamo published a memoir of his father and a poetry collection (Vento de Sal) that reflects on his poetic lineage. In these poems the poet refers to the public and familial losses of the times: 'We were all a bit lost then. / The dormant air of needling coal / and the blood stench / from the pockmarked plaza' ('Ali vivimos todos un pouco desnortados'); and the frontiers of memory: 'I try to grasp the country of your time / that I'll never enter' ('Pai de antiga profesion'). Chus Pato goes a step further than other poets in these anthologies in her critical engagement with Greek myth, and in her examination of the place of the poet of a minority language. In her introduction, Palacios describes Pato as a poet of transgression who works against genre in large-scale formats: 'that engage in a profound mutation of poetic discourse, that unearth formerly silenced voices, and that explore the limits between the speakable and the unspeakable'. In Pato's poems, the poet sets sail, her vocation agonic and undomesticated: 'savage it is that humanity speaks the words / savage it is the attention with which you listen' ('"*as sibilas somos Xeografia*"'). In 'Fisterra' the poet leaves the land behind, inhabiting subjectivity beyond community: 'that can't be tied down and, unspeakable, gains (psyche, life) the ends of the Earth, that imagines itself a ghost among many and marries the multiple organs of the land to the Land's End where dreams, ideologies, pnuemas, the dead are all cracked? What politics, beyond the crowd, beyond the flag, where the breath cracks'. Under the current paradigm, readers must translate for themselves the contradiction of reading this in a volume published with the support of the Galician Secretariat General of Culture, with funding provided by that perfect Tory tax on addiction, the Lottery Fund.

If these anthologies are anything to go by, as far as the nationalist aspirations of Spain's minorities are concerned, Catalonia is not going anywhere, the Basque Country will keep on getting the most out of things as they stand, while the Galicians, in their own minds, have already left. The literature of a minority is always an assertion in the face of repression. To seek out minority language poetry in translation is to be *decentred*. Given the current rise of illiberal nationalism around the world, such a reading practice might also be an exercise in *decency*, an aptitude in response to violent certitudes. Reading this way also requires a kind of *descent* from the preeminent position that English occupies in the global literary marketplace, to an encounter at the same level. Person to person contact (in the plaza, on the page) can be both disorienting and enlivening. In this space you might get ripped off; you might learn something.

Five Poems

MANUEL VILAS

Translated from the Spanish by James Womack

The Rain

Madrid, 22 May 2004

On the TV screens in the bars in Actur, Zaragoza
we saw the '53 Rolls with its white wheels
(fifty years; only a thousand kilometres on the clock).
I was holding a glass of cold white wine,
and Spain was already heating up;
the Mediterranean hotels were being spring-cleaned,
rooms all opened, fastidious chambermaids all waiting
for the arrival of six hundred thousand Englishmen,
a million Germans, four hundred thousand French,
a hundred thousand Swiss and a hundred thousand Belgians.
We had white wine in our hands and our necks
craned towards the TV set.

Elizabeth II of England did not come; Elizabeth II
would only accept an invitation to the King of France's wedding
and Elizabeth II, as France has no King,
stays now and forever in her palace, leaning back against the world.
It is Elizabeth II's subjects who love the Spanish sun and cheap beer,
who hang out the British flag
in their bars by the seaside.

Crepuscular royal houses, plucked
from the rustiest corners of history
appeared on Spanish televisions on 22 May 2004:
Nordic countries, distant and wealthy, cold and cut off
from this ever-embracing welcoming heart.
Rouco Varela leading the mass.
The President of the French Republic did not come.

The archbishops, two-tone, happy.
The Lord's name spoken out loud many times.
This obstinate obsession with naming God, naming Him
as one might give a name to power, or money,
or the Resurrection, the guillotine, prison, slavery.
The Emperor of the World stayed in America,
uninterested in the minor rituals of his provinces.
The huge blue umbrellas.
                                        To get up at six o'clock in the morning
so they can put on makeup, depilate you, give you a manicure:
what a joy.
The vast breakfasts, the silver cutlery,
the finest wines and the extraordinary colognes.
The gigantic shower-rooms, the suites, the Swiss chocolates,
the golden slippers, the platinum underwear,
the orange juice made from vile oranges.
Luxury and service, people always opening doors for you.
Permanent smiles.
The professionals with their permanent smiles,
smiles that represent the most inhospitable job in history.
Smile? What for?

And Umbra, and Gala, and Bosé, and A., and J., and Ayala, and M. M.
all walking into the Catedral de la Almudena,
rewarded, chosen,
seated on the right, the preeminent figures of Spanish *savoir-faire*,
of Spain's ascent, of its great growth.
The great ascent, the great ascension.
And the hundred and ninety people burnt alive had their homage paid them:
this absurd and mutilated populace, this Goyaesque populace
both elemental and monarchist.
The Rolls passed in front of them.
And the former President of the Republic drank a '94 Rioja Reserva;
all of the former Presidents of Spain, each with his jacket,
and his wife in the background,
protective, ravenous, eternally
interchangeable, but happy to have made it this far,
so far, all the way here where the air is gold and your hand can grasp the world,
here, this spot where the whole of Spain wanted to be
and democratic legitimacy is an absolute blazon.

Iridescent sun-hats, yokes on people's heads,
yokes under a darkening sky.
And José María Aznar and Jordi Pujol
and Felipe González, together again.
And the three of them felt happy to see a job well done,
Franco's succession, the European hand, paternal,
laid on our heads,
Franco's succession, the Francoist *mantillas*
put away in wardrobes,
screeching with envy and breathing the whitest naphtha.
And Juan Carlos I stuck carrying Spain,
because who would carry Spain if he did not,
who would carry Spain's history, the papal ring on his little finger.
And Zapatero with his wife Sonsoles, voluptuous, smiling,
the kind of woman who would have suited Baudelaire or Julio Romero.
Sonsoles looked like a Delacroix:
a close-fleshed Liberty guiding the people;
show-off sun-hats, the political ritual,
the boredom of history,
sagging tits.

And socialists and liberals and ultramontanes all together,
the left and the right muddled together,
salaries all expanded to satiety,
everyone looking for the same thing; Sonsoles looked like a Delacroix,
the new Queen of Spain,
Queen of doling out offices, of glories,
of long trips across the world in official aircraft,
of irreligious fortunes.
Atheists transformed in the blaze from the sun-hats,
believers with atheist wallets.
Power at all times always equal to itself.
Human history throughout time similar to how it was a while back.
The same time at all times.
The essence of Spain repeating itself, the essence of the wide world.

And all of us drinking in Actur, next to the cranes and the supermarket,
happy they allow us to drink this wine,
this cold wine, from a half-clean glass, happy
to have the money for this wine and then two more.

And the abused pallor of Queen Rania of Jordan.
And the rain.

Cocaine

Light of the city we drink you at night.

We make love so close to the kitchen –
this flat is so small –
that the smell of the drains comes through like an odour of sanctity,
dirty and sticky,
crooked, synthetic,
too hot...
all over your body with its tattoos and fishscales.

Light of the city you are white as the sun.

I know people, fifty-five years old or thereabouts,
in important jobs under the city lights:
people who speak perfect Spanish;
contented people with a position in society,
who never make love like you and I make love
(if this is love and not a lie),
with these cries forced from us
(if they are cries rather than stories):
these cries forced from our skin, our language, from the acid
of these enigmatic tiles on the floor;
I know people who barely love like this, as we do –
with anger and no future, rage and no compassion –
and I do not understand how life could be other
than the white hair
on your hypocritical and regally unconcealed flesh
as though the national anthems of France and Germany,
Russia and Spain, of Sweden, of Finland,
were blaring out not in any Olympic Games
but rather in the heart of these industrial suburbs.

Light of the city we drink you at night.

Sometimes we do not sleep in the small hours and think of Mars
and think of the ashes rising from the crematoria

(carbonised bodies, people born to decorate the sky
and seeking their grave in the contaminated air,
the air filled with human ashes rising from the ground:
tongues and arses, femurs and sacra, livers and semen);
we spend seven solid hours looking at the gilded rosette in the ceiling
of a bedroom doused in the noises
of ancient, faraway cars,
or of our neighbours opening and closing their doors;
and we look out of the window,
sensing through the frame
the strength of the cranes that build life and history.

Light of the city I drink you defenceless.

When I am seventy,
cut me wide open,
and throw my heart to the dogs.
And you, eat with them,
fight with them to let you sink your teeth in,
bite it like you know how,
bitch,
bite my heart.

I love you.

I love you so much.

I love you
like dinosaurs love the light that falls from stars,
love to drink it at night;
like lions in Africa gorge themselves on zebras with their dirt-filled kidneys;
like white men eat blacks with their hearts filled with white men's dreams.

Light of the city, you are my lover, my mirror, my joy.

I spend my nights screaming.
Against the darkness, against the moon,
screaming.
Take your clothes off, you dog:
screams in the small hours of the night,
in the stairwells of terrible apartment blocks:
praise, far too much praise.

Everything is white.

Take your clothes off, you dog. Are you shivering? Do I scare you?

Light of the city we drink you at night.

Light of the city that illuminates
the dogs,
the blacks,
the children,
the saints,
the resurrected,
the old,
the poor,
the murderers,
the women,
the unilluminable women.

Light of the city we drink you at night.

Light of the city over your *aschenes Haar Shulamith*.

Tonight I want so much.
I'll kill you. I'll give it you. I'll give you this.
We'll get married. I'll give it you, I swear.

I love you.

A Hundred Years Later

Madrid, June '98

No, you look, look at all the life here, look as much as you want.
Look at the cities filled with slaves, with wretched men.
I am just a student of philosophy
about to do the state exam, who spends his summer reading,
slowly, all of your books.
I never went to Germany, although I did learn Greek –
but I forgot it; I forgot it because I had to find a way
to earn a living: now it is thinking that supports me.
And I am here, in a room,
facing your thousands of words, words that no one believes in,
ruined words, words that will help me, if I remember them well,
to win a spot as a teacher in a provincial school
somewhere in Spain, in a country that you – I'm sure you had your reasons –
that you did not care to visit, to know, to travel across, to put your finger into.
No, believe me, there are no Spanish geniuses
in this philosophy textbook.

I was in your country once, years ago, on a package tour:
my whole life has been done on the cheap, but I loved it like you said
we should love all that flows from us
in a constant exhalation; and I was not fooled,
and rejected all vice, all drugs, the sandals the slave wears.

The world, the world you fell in love with, is over:
nature is a ruined old dame, melancholic,
stinking and unpleasant;
the mountains threw out their guardian angels, who died;
life itself lost the will to live, and is sick,
bedridden in a nursing home.

A hundred years have gone by and you have not returned, you will never return;
you fucked up there, but knew you would fuck up: like a leisure-class
anarchist, like a raving bourgeois who inhales
a new, pagan and seditious immortality.

And tell me if that is not in itself the drama: you left
and have no reason to live again, trapped in the lie that is death;
how clumsy our desires are, and our thoughts, and our theories,
and the hours we spent on the hard thought that leads
to a single enormous utopia; and time went by, and your life went by as well.

And my life goes by, less stressed than yours, which is why I am here, today,
moaning about it. The Greeks came to you, the arrogant-in-will,
the death of God... and women, all of them in love with your cruel talent,
and you felt them up with the rough hand of Dionysus;
and then there was the pure disdain for everything that came before you,
everything derived from the most perfect minds of the past;
but what about me? What is left for me
apart from your work in paperback editions, with underlinings
where I thought I found something important: ideas that, tomorrow –
if I am lucky and they ask me about you
rather than about Aristotle, or Aquinas, or even poor old Kant –
I'll have to explain as though I were hard-working, prudent, honourable?

Thirty-Six Years Old

Stairs wear me out, it's hard to write, it's hard to sleep,
everything that inspired me in the past now seems a load of rubbish;
I like money, the Christmas holidays, public holidays, snow, sun;
there's not much difference between me and my good old dog Trajan, we grew up
together, and I have seen the spiritual essence of man's life
dragging itself like an old cripple down the street
in hope's very own Chinatown; I will start to turn into
an animal with no idols, no gods, no church, no brothers,
like Trajan himself, who with every day is happier, more truly a dog.

The whole of life steps forward one morning at the end of July.
I am reading a book and at my side there's a glass
of white wine, yesterday's newspaper on the table,
and I'm listening to Lou Reed who is singing something like
what I am writing. My joints ache:
it must be the bloody mattress that is getting old and that I
should change, Jesus, how much does a new mattress cost?
My back hurts, my eyes, my left foot;
when I tell my mother I'm a bitter old man she gets scared;
when I tell one of my made-up friends –
like Florencio, who appears in some of my novels –
that I'm a shrivelled old mummy, he says no, I'm just on edge,
it's my imagination, my thought getting hard payback
from my body. How discreet middle age is, how false
the indications time gives us, how vain is human blood.
What a hypocrite I am, I who am not even old.

I'm going to have a shower right now, shave, brush my hair,
go out into the street clean and in fresh clothes, brand new trousers,
brand new shoes and a shirt, I'll try to be happy all night long
as I go from bar to bar, chatting to the anonymous boys and girls
 – I too am anonymous, a Black man, a Chinese, a dried-out Gypsy – ;
and I will pray and drink simultaneously, and at dawn, if I have not found
a loose (very loose) Filipina woman to love me, I will go home,
filled with fame and death, filled with light.

Let the Lord God number me among the saints; I have just
turned thirty-six; I like films about guns and aliens,
I like ten-thousand peseta notes, I like doing nothing,
I like to pray for the life I have led
And for the days to come, the New Year's Eves, the birthdays,
holidays by the sea and retirement and a cheap headstone;
I like expensive cars, the folk art
of Pedro Páramo; I like women – black women, white women;
I like trees, olives, trips to Cuba,
famous restaurants, high boots that squeak when you walk,
sharp knives, mountains, all the sad oceans and the moon.
Someone who has lives a little and been around,
like in a good film, will say, 'Fuck you, spic',
and my hand will be steady as I put a bullet through his throat.

Insomniac Memories

How perfect you were in the dawn light lying on the sofa
in my room, naked, smoking, reading a magazine;
your lips red, smiling like you were extremely wealthy:
I inherited a lot of money from my Swiss uncle, you said at dinner.

A woman who travels the world, lover of beaches and good weather,
made of light, terrifyingly young; *you will never grow old*
I said to you, and you: *kiss me here, on my hands, among the rubies*;
I shall, I replied, *isn't this suite big, how beautiful the sea*
when the dawn comes in; she said *I like the South, although everything bores me*,
and we did it once again, standing by the window, with our hands
on the windowsill, me taking her from behind; *how old are you?*
You'd like me to say eighteen, but I'm past thirty.
The music was the *Cabaret* soundtrack, and it was already hot.

Then, still naked, you looked at yourself in the suite's horrible mirror
and said, *come here, come close, choose a part of my body,*
whichever you want; pass me a cigarette, call room
service, call the airport, I want to go to Paris.
And I: *It's better to go to Stockholm, or Helsinki, somewhere cold,*
far away from this impatient summer, and you: *come here, choose a part*
of my body, anywhere, choose anywhere in the world, kiss me slowly.
I once killed a man; I could kill you too.
And I said *I've always wanted to be killed by a woman like you, I've lived*
long enough; do it now, I won't move a muscle,
I promise; plan it while I take a shower; a good crime.

And she kissed me again. *No, you kill me; I've had a lot of love;*
kill me with your hands, I need nothing from you,
but I could be your slave, you are so beautiful sometimes –
that lip, that hand, that noble gesture, that hard soul,
this silence: it all makes you covetable. You covet from me
the same as I do from you, the secret of what we were, and this secret
that made us love each other tonight; go now, I hope we never meet again.
Yes, I really hope so, let me look at you again; I cannot touch you,
I am ruined; I could fuck another man right now,
you get me? Life made us inexhaustible by nature:
go now; I want to sleep for a while and forget about you.

Imagine that just you and I were left on this planet,
and that we were back in the year 1,000 BC,
and that there were no roads or cities or states or governments,
but rather caves and villages, wooden houses by the river, and a vast moon
on summer nights; think about that while you're asleep.

Four Poems

ROD MENGHAM

liquidas orasse sorores

Of bodies reassigned, I sing
long before Ovid and his pack of lies

when the Bosphorus was welded shut
one last time, and you could walk
from Greece to Turkey against the traffic.
Now there is nowhere to cross
so we sail away, into the soapy water
of your absence. And I surprise myself
with this shipping manifest.

I thump out a tune and drive myself mad
very close to your location. Unless you are
the census-taker of dreams
or the functionary who
sees death in his board game.

Do we not bleed, are we not prone to bruising.

The psalmist tells us how God pushes him aside
like the fridge door in a poem about plums
where everything is gleaming tirelessly.

I, Tibullus Libertus Venusti, have taken an oath
to be more precise. I miss God enormously
but will take the first comer. I have learned
how to balance grief with payday. It is a gift I have

and this poem just kills me.

Pyx Path

On a January morning, on Malvern Hills, I was standing in a cloud moving north when a magpie alighted on my kit, declaring the beginning of the end. The rain dropping from the branches made the sound of a stream. The wind made the sound of flapping robes. For some reason we don't yet understand, very little has changed.

Down on the patios of Great Malvern, a squall whips the canapés off the table. First is food, the dread delight, the body of belief. When they go to bed, they leave the TV on all night, like corpse candles.

Led by an invisible hand, the endless grey cloud moves towards the event horizon, somewhere nearer Wales. I picture the foundries, with all their fires going out; and further west the tide, with its huge scintillations, beginning to turn.

Now the fog is laden with smoke from the next county. There is a faint ditch and bank at the base of North Hill. There is a faint disc barrow on Table Top Hill. The ancient track is lined with clover. The ditch is choked with silverweed. High in the elder, on a twisted branch, the magpie turns to curse the day. His is the call of the chainsaw. It cuts through a silence of grounded larks.

The Land of Cockayne

I'm on top of the world with blood all around
there are four springs and a line of poplars
on the planet's rim being borne along

without stint. The book in my hand disappears
and I rid myself of the drone of the past
but an overpowering need to look back

far out to sea, to the West of Spain
shows nothing left but cinders afloat
no halls nor bowers to scan.

I have waited too long
for the release mechanism
there is nothing in Paradise, nothing there

but burst water mains, ever flowing
like innate ideas of Brexit.

Drearily, drearily, shall we go
the song hangs heavy in the air
on a winter's night say I love you

to no-one. The words will rise like smoke
from the page, and find their own way home.
See the swarm flying from west to east

where is no night and only day
thanks to emergency floor lighting
whose glow unsteady like alabaster

is fixed in the bed of a northerly stream.
There even gravity loses heart
as the stones arise from their deepest sleep

and break, break, break,
in the seas off Dogger.

The Deserted Province

those are not the colours of the dawn
but the painted breasts of Iceni women
as fierce and stubborn as sap

before I lose you   the flames flicker
the throat tightens   and a million atmospheres
hit the central nerve

within the radius of the passing moment
you see the world reduced to a powder
that floats through the air like cheap scent

what am I afraid of   the dark
threading the needle of the lightning rod
the cold hands   the cold lips

courtesy of a black box
there is no spirit who walks beside you
only a coincidence and its shadow

we all walk slowly into solitude
a blind colossus in an exiled land
each eye turned into stone

your body is a temple cleared of thought
is my only thought
when push comes to shove

where do we disappear to
in the wild woods   you are on a flight path
to the hinges of the tulip

and the stars in the near distance
give you credit   for the snail's lustre
over the flagstones

with a sudden drop in air pressure
these are the twists of spring
the rhythmic debate of food and form

otherwise it's a town   it's a myth
and it's all those divisions
under one roof

better one moment in April
in blinding white and amarynth
with the crows scolding each to each

the skylark just barely screaming

An Affinity with Duck

John Goodridge and Bridget Keegan (eds), *A History of British Working Class Literature*
(Cambridge University Press) £79.99; Nicholas Cole and Paul Lauter, *A History of
American Working-Class Literature* (Cambridge University Press), £79.99

ANDREW HADFIELD

THERE'S SUCH A FASCINATING STORY to tell about traditions of working-class literature and culture and so many questions to ask that it is a surprise the histories are not mapped out more often. Is 'working-class literature' imagined and conceived by the middle and upper classes and so has to be judged in terms of more general conceptions of literature? Or is it a canon apart which is written to be consumed by the class from which the producers have emerged and so has separate standards and rules? To what extent should we think about working-class literature in terms of popular culture? As the editors of the American volume point out, 'working-class cannot simply' be thought of like race and gender as it is 'not usefully understood strictly as a category of identity', one reason why there has been so much more academic work on those issues in relation to literature than class. Of course there are connections that need to be made. In her pithy and astute 'Foreword' to the British volume Donna Landry points out that, 'The democratization of the literary marketplace that made professional literary livelihoods possible and allowed women to publish also benefitted the lower classes. Even the rural poor might occasionally find a voice through networks of patronage and publicity'. It is a pity that someone who has written so brilliantly on literature, class and the countryside has only a short piece here.

As many of the more astute commentators on contemporary society have argued in magazines and broadsheets, the current tendency to bandy about lazy conceptions of 'the white working class' make little sense (as well as being racist) because neither are homogeneous categories that explain anything. The aim is invariably to invoke a notion of 'white trash' or 'chavs' who cannot acquire the higher feelings of toleration and inclusiveness enjoyed by people in wealthier socio-economic brackets. Class, as Cole and Lautier put it, 'though it is manifested in daily life and in culture, has more to do with structural conditions of work, property, and ownership than with pigmentation, bodily configuration, assumptions about gender, nationality, and ethnic identification, or even with the deadly realities, historical and current, of racism, sexism, and other forms of bigotry'. Slightly ponderously expressed perhaps, but that is always the danger with writing about class, and the point has to be made.

The two books are relatively light on coherence and definitions and have all the strengths (and weaknesses) of the essay collection. There is an impressive range and diversity of material and approaches covering the emergence of British working-class culture and literature from the eighteenth century and American from the nineteenth. The standard of the essays is largely very high indeed, and I cannot think of any that do not perform some useful intellectual work even if it is in elaborating material that few readers will know well. Many cover a series of writings and can be largely descriptive in nature; others are more focused and analytical, explaining how particular texts and forms work. The American volume is especially good on race and slavery and their relationship to class; working class writers were sometimes astute about the relationship between race and class, sometimes tone deaf, especially if, like Jack London, they were in the grip of Darwinian theories about racial progress. The British volume is strong on the often pernicious effects of the celebrity culture of 'authentic' working-class writers, and has some especially impressive essays on class in the eighteenth century, and the relationship between the London printing presses and Welsh and Scottish writers.

Of course, given the vast variety of working-class culture and writing and the complicated history of class over the centuries this miscellaneous approach is easy to justify. Indeed, it was not that long ago that people imagined that class might be coming to an end and would not be a category that we would need to think about much in the future. Does anyone still read Francis Fukuyama's best-selling polemic, *The End of History and the Last Man* [sic] (1992), which argued that the West had won as the Soviet bloc collapsed, and Marxism became a historical relic? The story leaves out the rise of China, which obviously complicates that simple post-Cold War narrative. Fukuyamaesque commentators made the further mistake of assuming that because so much discussion of class was intimately linked to Marxism, Marxism had come to equal a belief in the significance of class, and vice versa. And, if one thinks more parochially, there was also a strange notion that because class explanations of past events had failed so dismally – e.g., the once widespread notion that the 'English' civil war was a battle between royalist cavaliers and bourgeois roundheads – class was a modern phenomenon precipitated by the Industrial Revolution, which had no bearing on the periods before.

Leaving class out of the story is always a risk, given how important a feature of everyday life for almost everyone it has always been. Imagining that 'class' only has meaning once cities, mechanised production and industrial poverty appear often results in a naïve belief in the rural idyll of 'Merrie England'. One of the dominant motifs of literary criticism until well into the 1980s was T. S. Eliot's claim in his essay 'The Metaphysical Poets' (1921) that in the Renaissance poets 'possessed a mechanism of sensibility which could devour any kind of experience', linking thought and feeling, as in the poetry of John Donne. It is not much of a stretch to see such arguments bathed in a nostalgia for a world before the

Enlightenment, modernity and class reared their ugly heads and separated everything out. No longer was poetry as natural as eating an apple, science a part of everyday life, and the lord of the manor and his grateful tenants united in their shared religion. Instead there was frosty analysis, atheism and nasty class conflict.

It is something of an irony that the American volume goes back further than the British, opening with a thoughtful essay by Matthew Pethers on transportation narratives and colonial literature in the seventeenth century. It is hard to have much working-class literature when the vast majority of the population were illiterate, but a conceptual opening dealing with the seventeenth century might have been a good move. Instead the British volume opens with a neat, thoughtful piece by Jennie Batchelor on labouring women writers in eighteenth-century England based on research in the archives at the Foundling Hospital in Coram Fields, London, exploring the range of foundling petitions written as the impoverished had to leave their children to be cared for by an institution. Often these petitions take on the form of 'seduction ballads', a mother adopting the narrative of a fallen woman, the victim of a dishonest or weak suitor, sacrificing herself for her child. Therefore they need to be read in terms of literary models which means that if we are deaf to the nature of these petitions and demand that they be read in terms of dominant literary categories 'we risk privileging elite discourses of value around aesthetics or sexual politics of class' (p.22). It is a powerful plea and asks the central question that the collection poses: how should we read and value working-class writing?

I will largely concentrate on the chapters which analyse poetry in the volume for readers of this journal. The next essay by Jennifer Batt is one of the stand-out pieces, exploring the impact of Stephen Duck (c.1705–56), the 'thresher poet', much favoured by Queen Caroline, who gave him the cushy job of showing people around her literary grotto. Duck is a strange and fascinating figure in literary history: should we see him as the authentic voice of the labouring writer? Or a pampered and isolated lackey, plucked from obscurity to satisfy the curiosity – and possibly guilty feelings – of the upper classes? Duck's poem, 'The Thresher's Labour' was answered by Mary Leapor (1722–46) with 'The Woman's Labour', who showed how his disparaging comments about women workers in his literary account of the year of an agricultural labourer obscured the hard work of rural women. As Batt points out, Duck's example inspired a wealth of poetry by labouring class writers, some of it genuine; some of it faked by unscrupulous publishers and grub-street hacks recognising the chance of making a quick buck; some of it satirical. Surprisingly enough, the authors 'Arthur Duck', 'James Drake' and 'Stephen Goose' turn out to be pseudonyms, 'their claims designed to mock, rather than participate in, the scrabble for patronage which the Queen's bounty to the thresher was feared to have unleashed'.

Duck's impact was powerful and ambiguous. On the one hand it inspired people who did not usually have their poetry published to write and helped them reach a wider audience; on the other, it encouraged some awful verse and provided an in-built excuse: 'To declare affinity with Duck was not just to assert novelty; it also allowed

one to claim an excuse for any defects a reader perceived in one's verse'. Batt's essay raises questions which are as important as those in Batchelor's essay: when does the invocation of class become a cynical exercise which actually serves to bolster rather than challenge the status quo? Recent examples – in particular the dispute over the value of the work of Kate Tempest and Holly McNish – spring to mind. Duck's fame 'shaped what it meant to be a labouring class writer in the 1730s', but it is not clear that his example changed literary culture, perceptions of value, or class.

William Christmas's essay on the verse epistle in the wake of Duck supplements and reinforces many of Batt's points. It contains a deft analysis of Mary Leapor's response to Duck's denigration of women, showing how, despite her claims to be an uneducated woman, she uses her understanding of poetic traditions to represent a golden age when women enjoyed equal status with men as they worked together in the fields:

> When Men had us'd their utmost Care and Toil,
> Their Recompense was but a Female Smile;
> When they by Arts or Arms were render'd Great,
> They laid their Trophies at a Woman's Feet;
> They, in those days, unto our Sex did bring
> Their Hearts, their All, a free-will Offering;
> And as from us their Being they derive,
> They back again should all due Homage give
> (cited on pp. 47–8).

Collier, who died from measles when only twenty-four, was well-received by readers. Her work seeks to overturn the assumptions of male labouring poets, but, as this extract indicates, she relied on the same pastoral conventions. John Clare, probably the most celebrated of all labouring class poets, also wrote in terms of the georgic and the pastoral as well as personal observation, as Gary Harrison points out in his essay.

The volume is attentive to differences in conceptions of class throughout the British Isles as the brilliant essay by Mary-Ann Constantine demonstrates. She asks whether labouring class poetry in Wales differs from that of the equivalent phenomenon in England and what happens when the traditions meet. She analyses the career of Edward Williams, a Welsh-speaking Glamorgan stonemason who launched a career in English announced in *The Gentleman's Magazine* in 1789. The poet was represented as 'sober and temperate', existing on a vegetable diet and, being naturally reserved, living the life of a hermit. However, the use of the word 'genius' shows that what we have here is 'a master class in melding the fundamental elements of what one might term the "English" concept of the "labouring class poet" with a more exotic Welsh "bardic" persona', one that persisted well beyond the eighteenth century. Welsh labouring class poets were forced to work within two language traditions, and, as Constantine points out, if we want to understand the nature of literature and class 'in these islands', we will need to get to grips with the different traditions and the ways in which they interact.

With the onset of the Industrial Revolution poetic conventions and horizons changed. Mike Sanders provides an astute reading of *The Purgatory of Suicides* (1845) the extraordinary poem by the Chartist, Thomas Cooper (1805–92), written in nine hundred and sixty-three Spenserian stanzas while he was in prison. The poem is a direct challenge to prevailing orthodoxies and hierarchies by retelling a series of stories from classical history and literature in order to 'democratise "elite" knowledge', demystifying what had been the preserve of the privileged. Historical actors never really understood the significance of their actions and the truth will appear as history unfolds in a rational manner and becomes clear to all:

> What though these words, like oracles of old,
> Were sealed, in their full meaning, to the seer
> Who uttered them? – The future shall behold
> Their splendid verity
> (cited on p.238).

Cooper, according to Sanders, is an unusual example of a 'working-class writer living by virtue of his intellectual labor while largely avoiding the compromises associated with either patronage or Grub Street' (p.246).

Kirstie Blair also shows how important it is to consider the mode of publication and the relationship between the author and the means of dissemination in her essay on the Victorian newspaper. If we only explore anthologies and the familiar modes of publication – which were not usually read by working-class readers – we will miss most working-class poetry because virtually all of it was published in broadsheets. Perhaps the most important poet of recent years who explores his working-class roots in his work is Tony Harrison. Jack Windle contributes a thoughtful essay on Harrison's thinking about race and class in his work, and his desire to foreground the 'democratic multiculturalism' (Paul Gilroy's terms) of the British working class as a counter to claims that ordinary people are generally racist. Windle analyses Harrison's sympathetic debate with his ageing father's sense of isolation and alienation in increasingly multi-cultural Leeds, and his extraordinary reworking of Gray's 'Elegy Written in a Country Churchyard', 'V' (1985), in which the author confronts his alter-ego, the skinhead who defaced his parents' tombstones. The poems are written against the background of the devastating effects of 'chronic unemployment and social disintegration in Thatcher's Britain':

> *What'll t'mason carve up for their jobs?*
> *The cunts who lieth 'ere wor unemployed?*
> ('V', cited on p. 364).

The 'afterword' is written by Brian Maidment who was asked because he edited a pioneering anthology of '"self-taught" nineteenth-century poets', published by Carcanet in 1987, which has, as the author gratefully acknowledges, been in print ever since.

The American volume acknowledges that we now live 'in a time of extreme class inequality' which means it is urgent that we consider the 'historical contexts within which working-class literature was formed: colonization, slavery, the industrial revolution, repeated economic depressions, wars hot and cold, deindustrialization, globalization... and capitalism'. The order of this list is significant and Matthew Pethers argues that class in

America, a colonial society built largely on slave labour, has always been intertwined with race, a point supplemented at greater length in John Ernest's, Bill Mullen's and other essays, while John Marsh shows how desperate attempts were made to persuade the working classes that they had nothing in common with slaves to prevent a dangerous collection response of people with mutual interests. A founding text of American literature is Defoe's *Moll Flanders* (1722), inspired by the story of Moll King, a pickpocket transported to Virginia in 1718. Both Molls were formed and made by their American experiences, Moll F. able to return to England a wealthy woman after making good in a slave-owning society and in another novel, Defoe's protagonist, Colonel Jack, empathises with black slaves when his adventures place him amongst them. But if the origins of the novel opened a window for working-class writers it was soon closed as the history of the form shows that it was almost exclusively produced and consumed by the middle-classes.

Paul Lautier provides an important and thoughtful essay on the nature of work, which points out how the question, 'For whom are you working?', was central to the development of American notions of class structure and identity, the ideal being a mode of independence and self-sufficiency. Lautier argues that this ideal has hobbled attempts at more collective action in the United States, writers such as Orestes Brownson able to identify the issues of slavery and class oppression but not having the intellectual resources or tradition to provide a credible solution, turning in the end to Christian ideals of moral behaviour as a way of combating the influence of 'priests, banks, and monopolies'. Herman Melville's 'Bartleby' is 'clearly a story about work under capitalism', the refrain that he would prefer not to leading to an impasse rather than a way forward. Peter Riley's essay on Whitman reinforces this argument and makes a striking connection between two giants of nineteenth-century writing more often contrasted than aligned. Whitman always represented himself, in images as well as his verse, as a 'free man' and opposed slavery on the grounds that it infringed 'America's smallholding pledge to "each Young Man in the Nation, North, South, East, and West"', rather than 'as a response to human suffering'. The volume is full of stories of the desire not to think about class, with Amy Schrager Lang arguing that in the antebellum novel the moral is invariably that 'gender trumps class'.

There is more on prose in the American volume, which contains many excellent essays which should make many popular and influential works visible once again. Alicia Williamson shows that in socialist fiction written before the First World War (an important sub-genre when the Socialist Party leader, Eugene Debs, was riding high in the polls) marriage is the solution to inequality rather than its opposite, and a means of heading off 'the lusty atavistic violence of anarchists' (p.153). Michael Collins writes incisively on the ways in which life writing was encouraged by contemporary anthropological theory to make working-class autobiographies into expressions of 'a historicized group life' (p.200), an 'authenticity' imposed on the lower classes. As Michelle Tokarczyk points out, innovative writers like Muriel Rukeyser (1913–80) were able to overcome the artificial dichotomy between 'socially conscious versus experimental writing' (p.259).

There are some good essays on more recent poetry. Richard Flacks has a useful overview of 'The American Labor Song Tradition', explaining the importance of Yip Harburg's still moving 'Brother, can you spare a dime'. Cary Nelson explores the poetry of work to the end of the Cold War, which – yet again – shows how race and class cannot be separated in the American tradition through his reading of Melvin Tolson's *Libretto for the Republic of Liberia* (1953), which he considers alongside Ginsberg's *Howl* (1956).

These two volumes, along with Michael Pierce's *A History of Irish Working-Class Writing*, also published by Cambridge last year, were planned and co-ordinated by Ray Ryan, an excellent example of a publisher working alongside academics to produce much-needed and innovative books. All involved in those projects deserve our praise for putting in plain sight work which should never have been obscured.

Selected extracts from
The Iliad *in Birmingham Hexameters*[1]

Sam Trainor

Oi, Goddess, sing us a song, bab: that one about Achilles,
Peleus's mardy nipper, who got a proper cob on,
Causing all kinds of grief for his brave Achaean muckers.
Shed loads of souls got sent to Hades thanks to face-ache –
It was all-you-can-eat dead meat for the carrion crows and stray dogs.

I. Thetis weedles a favour out of Zeus (1:493–530)

Twelve nights had passed since the barney, and just as morning was breaking,
All the immortals were wending their way back to Olympus,
Zeus at the head of the crew. Thetis had not forgotten
What she'd promised her son, so up from the sea she floated,
Rising to heaven at dawn, and climbed to the top of Olympus.
There she found beady-eyed Zeus, son of Kronos, sitting,
All on his tod, on one of the mountain's highest ridges.

Kneeling in front of him, cuddling his knees with her left hand,
Stroking his chin with her right, Thetis pleaded with great Zeus:
'Godfather, I've always done you proud with the other immortals;
It's about time, mighty Zeus, that you returned the favour:
Stick your neck out for my son, the one who's doomed to die young.
King Agamemnon has robbed him, disrespected the poor boy,
Swiped his trophy girlfriend like a bit of plunder.
Now only Zeus can help him, wisest of the Olympians:
Throw all your weight behind the Trojans till the Argives
Show him the proper respect and pay him compensation.'

Thetis held out for an answer but Zeus wasn't saying sod all.
Head in the clouds as he sat there, playing his face, he kept schtum.
Thetis squeezed even tighter, trying again to cajole him:
'Give me your solemn promise, or nod your head or something,
Tell me to get lost, even. What do you care if Thetis finds out
Zeus couldn't give a monkey's about some lowly sea-nymph?'

Glowering Zeus looked miffed; he cleared his throat and grumbled:
'You're gunna get me in bother with her indoors, you know that?
Hera gets one whiff of this, I'm in for a tongue-lashing.
Every day she slags me off in front of the others,

Claiming I'm helping the Trojans win this blinkin battle.
You'd better hop it sharpish, in case she gets wind you were here.
Give me some time to mull it over; I'll get it dealt with.
Tell you what, I'll nod me head to show you I mean it.
Everyone knows a nod from the boss is a binding contract:
Never has Zeus gone back on his word if he's given the nod.'

Kronos's youngest furrowed his brow and lowered his forehead,
Swaying his natty dreadlocks, and all Olympus quivered.

II. HECTOR STICK AJAX, THE REMATCH (13:794–837)

Zeus was still egging em on, and in they steamed like gales
Battering down on the Earth beneath the Big Guy's thunder,
Whistling and whipping the seawater into a right palaver:
Towering breakers churning up the foaming ocean,
Hurtling headlong to shore, wave after frothy wave –
That's how the Trojans stormed on, wave after wave of bronze:
Gleaming warriors piling in – the posse and backup.

First up was Hector, Priam's kid, as hard as Ares,
Butcher of mortal men, he held out his big round shield –
Multi-layered leather, covered in rigid bronze-plate –
Over his temples a helmet, glinting as it shuddered,
Striding all over the shop, his shield up as he drove on,
Probing the line for a bit of give, or a point of weakness,
Failing to put the frighteners on the tough Achaeans.

Out stepped big Ajax, squaring up to him, and gave it,
'Hector, just do one will you. What d'you think you're playin at,
Trying to put the collywobbles up us Argives?
This int our first time round the block, you pranny.
Only old Zeus has been keepin us from battering you.
Banjaxing Greece's ships is what you've set your heart on;
Take it from me though, mate, we'll hold you off all day long.
Maybe you think you're hard, but we're tooled up and mob-handed.
Likelihood is, we come round your yard and we trash it.
As for you lot, pretty soon you're gunna peg it,
Praying to Zeus to make your horses, with their fancy manes,
Bomb back across the plain to Troy as fast as falcons;
Going like the clappers, trailing plumes of dust behind you.'

Over to Ajax's right, there was a soaring eagle
Gliding above as he spoke, and all the arrayed Achaeans –
Chuffed to have seen the omen – cheered, but up piped Hector:
'Ajax, you div, you ent half got a bob on yourself.
You're talking out the back of your bleedin neck.
What I wouldn't give to be only half as certain
Hera was me mom, and mighty Zeus my old man,
Everyone thinking the sun shone out my arse, like Apollo,
Like Athena, as I am that all you Argives
Cannot avoid the shitkicking you'll get today;
And you unall, you prick, if you take on my big spear,
My hefty shaft'll rip right through your lilly-white flesh.
Ilion's dogs and birds will scoff your brawn and chittlins;
Ajax'll serve up a feast by them ships when he kicks the bucket.'

Hector took up the charge, his backup roaring behind him,
All the Achaeans yelled back, not giving an inch to the Trojans,
Standing their ground against Ilion's hardest hitting fighters.
The total pandemonium the scrap created
Drifted right up to heaven, and to dazzling Zeus.

'Hector, my gorgeous boy, you'll always be my favourite.
Back when you were alive, the gods all doted on you;
Now that you're dead, it's not like they've hung you out to dry.
All of my other sons Achilles thrashed in battle,
Trafficked overseas, sold into slavery
In Samos, or in Imbros, or that rathole Lemnos.
This time, once his blade had carved out your last breath,
Over and over, he dragged your corpse all round the wrekin:
Turning rings around the grave of his buddy, Patroclus –
Not that it could ever bring him back, for gods' sakes –
Still, you look as fine as morning dew: fresh-faced,
Peaceful, like Apollo's pranged you with his soft darts.'

NOTES

1   'Birmingham Hexameters' is a phrase of Thomas De Quincey's. By 'Birmingham' he meant 'debased', 'artlessly faked'. He was comparing the shoddy verse produced by the Delphic oracle to the poetry of Sophocles, likening the aesthetic gulf to the disparity between the work of Stephen Duck, the thresher-poet, who was supposedly considered for the position of poet laureate in 1730, and his illustrious contemporary, Alexander Pope. It was, of course, Pope's enormously successful translation of the *Iliad* that was primarily responsible for him gaining the reputation as the first poet to make a fortune from selling his work. Twenty years after De Quincey's condemnation, Matthew Arnold sparked a brief fad for a synthetic version of epic dactylic hexameter as a means of translating Homer. Tennyson called this a 'burlesque, barbarous experiment', by which he meant something quite similar to De Quincey's 'Birmingham', though he later made extensive use of the verse form in his Lincolnshire dialect poems.

It is tempting to trace this use of 'Birmingham' to the electroplating industry that began turning out cheap imitation silverwork in the West Midlands during the 1840s. However, the term (and the whole tradition of nose-thumbing inauthenticity) dates to the Restoration period when the town's non-conformist metalworkers, who had supplied a good deal of parliamentary weaponry during the civil war, took to counterfeiting the King's coin as an act of covert rebellion. I trace my own work to this counter-cultural tradition.

So, by 'Birmingham Hexameters' I mean two things: Arnold's 'burlesque' epic hexameter, and the 'barbarous' vernacular of post-industrial Birmingham.

It Never Was in France or Spain

HORATIO MORPURGO

You are told a lot about your education but some beautiful, sacred memory,
preserved since childhood, is perhaps the best education of all.
from the epilogue to The Brothers Karamazov

THE POET SEÁN RAFFERTY and his wife Peggy kept a village pub in Devon for thirty years, retiring in the late 1970s. 'Seán' was a youthful tribute to the land of Yeats. Born 'John', in the Scottish Borders, he was educated at Edinburgh University but spent his adult life in England, rarely returning north. With his Scots origins, Irish adopted name and English adoptive home, it is tempting, in the midst of present multiple muddles, to cast him as the British riddle personified. He comes to mind for so many reasons at the moment.

I knew him best after he and Peggy retired to a house at the bottom of a farm track, a short walk across fields from my own childhood home. He could never remember how many times the BBC had sent a reporter to interview them at the pub about the death of the English village. He would check with Peggy in a little ironic double-act: 'How many times did the village die while we were there?'

In one context or another, that scepticism about overblown claims was a constant.

He'd read Classics at Edinburgh and was forbiddingly well-read. I didn't know what to say to him as a small child but that gradually changed and he acted as a kind of tutor-without-portfolio during my student years and for some time after. With my own world growing exponentially more complicated, I relied on him. The first issue of *PN Review* I ever read was the one he sent me in my third year at Cambridge with a selection of his poems, typos carefully corrected in biro. [*PNR* 26, 1982.]

Arched, bushy eyebrows with a tentative severity in the grey-blue glance. Baggy woollen jerseys and old corduroys of indeterminate hue; I never saw him wear anything but gardening clothes. He had the air of a retired priest by the time we had things in common, but in the thirties, just down from Edinburgh, he had hung about Soho with the best of them, writing songs and sketches for a musical theatre, getting erudite poems into magazines. His early work was well received by Hugh MacDiarmid and Sorely MacLean. In London he had called on and liked Edwin Muir, who liked him back and fixed him up with those little magazines. He had gone drinking with William Empson.

'Fitzrovia's replacement by the post-war Soho scene made him doubly a émigré. He was already Scottish in that on-the-run-from-Presbyterianism, reading-in-three-or-four languages way. In Devon he was, additionally, an exile from pre-war London. Scottishness definitely did still come into it but he was at several removes from belonging anywhere, or wishing to, so far as I could tell.

After Peggy died he stayed on alone at the cottage, continuing to run the vegetable garden for the children's farm my parents had set up. The house was next to a working dairy. As the cows were driven in on summer evenings, you could hear a strange scuffing as they dragged their tough hides along the outside of his living-room's cob wall, pushing and shoving their way towards the parlour. He enjoyed the gardening and was good at it but thirty years behind the bar of a village pub had inoculated him against all sentimentality about country life.

He'd grown up in the manse of a village in Dumfries, so this wasn't sniffiness about the provinces. Attachment to his native as to his adoptive countryside, both, is everywhere in the poetry: 'ancestral images / of dusk and peace and night: / the wild geese when they trace / over the Solway sky / an alphabet of flight.' Or from a late poem: 'there in the summer rain a heron will rise from the shallows / spreading great wings heavy with acclamation.' At the end he chose to have his ashes scattered on the river he haunted as a boy and we travelled up to see it done: 'Annan water wading deep / I shall lay me in a sleep / deeper than the Rochell.'

In the village he began with – long before TV had been thought of – literature supplied his precocious younger self with the larger views it craved. Tolstoy in French, Wordsworth, Scots Ballads. And that was, with modifications, the view he went on identifying with from this English spot 'between here and the next place', where life arbitrarily set him down in his thirties. Let the rural correspondents, in other words, search out whatever it is they mean by villagey-ness. Pockets of resistance to kitsch may be stumbled upon at the bottom of Devon lanes as elsewhere. Only metropolitan conceit imagines otherwise.

Ted Hughes was an old friend. With Seán, at least, the Poet Laureate in his later socialite phase knew what to expect when he boasted about fishing trips with cabinet ministers. And he got it. This was personal as well as political: Seán well remembered a younger Ted and the circle of writer friends with whom he would drink and talk literature in the pub. It didn't only worry him that the power elite was proving such a distraction from the poetry. He voiced criticism also of the animal and bird poems for which Hughes was and is famous. The creatures in those poems seemed to him 'heraldic'. Whether or not that was fair, it was an astute term, about animals as badges, as ruthless embodiments, especially given Hughes' penchant for the Conservative Party hierarchy.

Seán remained vigilant about what the Thatcher moment was trying then to foist on us as part of some immemorial natural order. That is also what comes to mind when I think of him now. And yet the hand-printed poem Ted had given him and signed, about eels, hung in its black frame on the inside of that wall which cattle dragged their hides along the outside of.

He had never owned a television and never left the country. What he had instead was a kind of literary Europe. He travelled either through books or letters. We corresponded often, for example, when I set off on my travels after leaving university. I started with Germany and found myself in the right place at the right time when the Berlin Wall fell that autumn. He read my accounts of those heady days and wrote back at length. I still come across his letters folded into the pages of the books I read then, often on his recommendation.

I wrote self-consciously from Gdansk, for example, about 'contemplating the Baltic' from a wind-swept beach on a chilly Easter weekend in 1990. He responded: 'sitting on my arse in Devon, your letter made me feel slightly dizzy.' If he'd gone to France himself, he often said, he couldn't have 'trusted himself to come back'. It was a revealing phrase. How was it he never, in all those years, went and had a look? It was not unusual for people of that generation never to go abroad, but was it normal for people who had taken that much trouble to learn about foreign cultures never to go?

Reluctantly he seemed to accept that in my case something needed to be worked through and physical restlessness was how I would do it. After a year or two, it's true, he did begin rolling his eyes as I outlined my next expedition. But he also referred me to Baudelaire's *The Painter of Modern Life*, about 'Mr G', the eternally mobile magazine illustrator – a forerunner of today's press photographer.

In the summer of 1992, just back from a disastrous American adventure, I escorted a coach-load of Czechs travelling to London from Northamptonshire, perhaps with a view to writing an article. The subject was newsworthy enough. They had just celebrated the first-ever twinning ceremony between an English and Czech town. But they then made the mistake of showing scant interest in my (high-minded) proposals for their day in London. Window-shopping on Oxford Street was their preferred option. Piqued, outraged, the revolutions of 1989 stood revealed to me now as a pitiable sham. I treated Seán to a full account of my disappointment the next time I was in Devon.

Scepticism about the overblown: he responded by reminding me of Ivan's discussion with Alyosha in *The Brothers Karamazov*. It was one of the books I'd read at his prompting. Their discussion is about how you can entertain comforting illusions about people from a distance but it's much harder to like people as they actually are. This was nothing to do, in other words, with the Cold War or the end of it. This problem is a permanent fixture. But that was lucky, too, in a way, because it meant there was help on hand from all those who have worked on it in the past.

I'm reminded so often of what a great teacher Seán was. Ivan, of course, is a journalist approaching thirty, who returns to his home town in a highly wrought state.

His younger brother, Alyosha, is a novice at the monastery there and they meet to discuss the different paths they have chosen. Thirty was still a long way off for me but their differences are not the kind you fully resolve at any age.

Another time he talked me through a short story of Hemingway's, *Soldier's Home*, about a young man who returns from the First World War to his hometown in the Mid-West. Some fuss is initially made of him, but the townspeople have meanwhile fed on a diet of atrocity as supplied by the newspapers. They soon lose interest in his version of events. He finds he can hold on to people's attention only if he starts 'telling unimportant lies'. So he starts claiming to have seen things that in fact other people saw. Little by little the inaccuracies add up, start rotting the truth about what the war had meant to him. Gradually the pretence takes over. 'In this way he lost everything,' the narrator drily comments.

I suppose it was obvious to me even then that this was Séan's way of trying to help. But do we ever really appreciate these things at the time? Ivan longs to visit Europe but knows that if he ever gets there he will surely be both filled with admiration for its past achievements and appalled by its present state. It helped to know that was an option. *Soldier's Home* is all about the nausea people can come 'home' to if they miss the way to relate truthfully what they have been through. Adapting your past to suit other people's expectations may seem harmless enough at the time but can lead to serious trouble later.

It wasn't suppressed spite – that he talked travel down because he'd done so little of it himself. He still occasionally translated from Greek and would recall the Regius Professor at Edinburgh arriving drunk to take his class through Book Six of the *Odyssey*. The storm-tossed Ulysses is cast upon the Phaeacian shore: 'This is where Western poetry begins,' his teacher had told them, sometime in the late nineteen twenties. And Séan repeating it to me now felt like inclusion in a community of sorts. Travel if you must, but only if it *means* something. *Faut-il partir? Rester? Si tu peux rester, reste. / Pars, s'il le faut.*

Was all this reading about it rather than doing it largely a function of being broke? Or for being chained to that pub and a difficult marriage? He was bisexual but quite unbothered who knew it, so everyone did. That must have had something to do with the 'slight angle' from which he viewed his life in this rural hetero-idyll. As a young man, the prospect of living with another man had seemed 'faintly ridiculous', he said, but he regretted now not having had the courage of his feelings.

He was a kind of displaced person in whom the displacement, the restlessness, had all been recast as a state of mind. His wasn't the kind he could ever have resolved by getting in a train let alone a plane. Scarcely imaginable now. But he *chose* to sit still with that restlessness. And so, from the end of an English farm track, he went on mocking Horace and quoting Sappho and referencing Hölderlin and echoing Donne.

He had a theory that the vagrant with whom De Quincey shared a room off Oxford Street when he ran away to London as a teenager was in fact a hallucination. This 'Anne', he thought, was produced under the pressure of De Quincey's isolation and drug addiction. The girl was a mental projection generated by his own dislocation and by the patron saint of Soho, Saint Anne.

The idea surely said as much about his own sacral hauntings as De Quincey's. When the upstairs rooms were tidied up after he died, he was found to have been living out of suitcases. One of his best poems is a translation from Italian about an African who has chosen to live in a cheap hotel in Paris and hardly himself knows why.

I know Europe is all about trade deals and the difference between a customs union and a free market. I know the suits and the lab coats long ago carved the continent up between them or are very soon expected to. Yes, the modernist literary Europe with which Séan tried to keep faith was already then out of date. The attempt left him penniless and unknown outside a small circle. But what I saw clearest, with his help, in those restless years of my own, was that he had not been routed. Quite the contrary: he had more to teach me then than anyone else I knew. He had not run away back 'home' anywhere and was, in his way, affirming me in my decision not to do so either. He had gained in 'heart-affluence' (he had time for Tennyson, too) what he might have lost in those forms of affluence which achieve a wider respect. I still think a Europe that is not re-made in the image of something like the conversation he believed in will fail. I still think that conversation is what Europe depends on, whether or not it is aware.

Séan died suddenly in 1993, so there was no moment when I knew I was saying goodbye. I think maybe he did know: the last time I saw him he gave me his old copy of George Herbert's poems. Which must be why *Quidditie* still sounds so much like him to me: *My God, a verse is not a crown, / No point of honour, or gay suit, / No hawk, or banquet, or renown, / Nor a good sword, nor yet a lute: / It cannot vault or dance or play, / It never was in* France *or* Spain...

Yet I'm forever just off to some 'France or Spain' or other. I still haven't learnt to settle the way Séan did. Years later, I came across an ancient Greek interpretation of the *Odyssey* Book Six. On this theory, Ulysses's arrival on Phaeacia should be read as an allegory. The scene is really code for the soul's return to its 'true country' across 'the dark ocean of the sensible life'. According to Porphyry, in the third century AD, Neptune's rage is provoked by the hero's abandonment of the material world, hence the storm he sends to wreck Ulysses. It is only with the assistance of divine courage that Ulysses 'encounters the billows of adversity, and bravely shoots along the boisterous ocean of life'. It's the kind of thing Séan would have enjoyed hearing and might well already have known.

Two Poems

BETSY ROSENBERG

Downtown

Lying on my back, knees up,
pressing lightly on my heels
suddenly it was 1950
on a downtown street in Cleveland, Ohio
and I was a slender young man in a
gray suit and gray fedora
outside an office building
about to
walk through a revolving door.

Under the concrete
is a world not gray but beautiful,
where I am at home among the bones
of Iroquois and Kickapoo, ho Kickapoo,
my brothers, my sisters

There is a cokey stench from
steel mills that light the sky red at night
before it snows
and I sense the stars,
a ghostly fragrance

the Cuyahoga river and the lake,
fallen leaves from
pawpaw trees,
sweet as anything,
beech and oak and aspen

Ho Grandpop, gazing up
at the red night sky,
man of steel, man of the sea,
may your bones rest easy in
Bet Olam, Hebrew house of all eternity

Balsam

Before that caravan approached
the walls of Jericho,
just as clouds were mantling
over the palms
a leaf from a balsam tree
fell into my chalice
and when I chewed it absently
I was filled with calm,
a calm so deep
I picked a sprig of balsam,
scraped a tear of resin
off the bark
and slipped them into a tiny pouch,
then sailed the wished-for river
of peace from here to Gaza
with a gift for you,
past greening groves,
the Queen's *afarsemon*.

Three Poems

CLAUDINE TOUTOUNGI

Chiaroscuro

Feeling of late even more
deracinated than usual

and finding a quartz, tinkly rosary in her father's old cigar box

she began to talk
privately in public places

parks, station platforms, open spaces, conscious with every
stone of how

she let herself be picked
up and put down often

and wishing for firmer categories

aware of being
neither the little angel

clinging to the off-white ankle of Christ

nor the shadowy Magdalene
slipping away

and not unhappy about this

(though some days to be
either blind or definitely a seer would be simpler)

she kept on

fumbling
towards salvation

as if you could muster it

as if you could force a miracle
out of the rushing air.

Apology, for Ayano

I am sorry I did not come through on the English conversation
after our first and only lesson. Winter here is hard. The cold –
interminable and I could not take the long walk across town into
sleet to reach your house. I admit I did not uphold my end of the
bargain. I should have nailed my colours to the mast where
you and where your baby Shunto could have seen them.
Ayano, I assure you – not all the people of this land are shilly
-shalliers, fobber-offers, shifty loons, curmudgeons, dolts,
prevaricators, poltroons, lugworms, shoddy planners, hags,
hogs, sots and shameful dilly-dalliers. Not all of us. Though
in the wintertime, I grant you, it may feel like more than some.

Rift

Pretend it's August. Pretend there's sunlight on bare arms, dappled
water, louche, marauding ducks.

Pretend the sheep wear serious faces, slouch in groins of gouged-out
rock and far-off human chatter's growing slack,

losing all heft until there's nothing on the breeze but buzzards
mewling. Nothing more incomprehensible than that,

nothing more consoling.

Three Poems

SUSAN DE SOLA

The Matchstick Man

takes great leaps
on his one pale leg.
Bounds with relish,
saltates with snap,

florid, russet-haired,
bulbed like a baster,
slubbed with sulfur.

He smiles dithyrambs,
ardent as a dog,
ecstatic to see me.

Suddenly, he leaps,
spins to a headstand,
grovels along the emery –

a long, intense
nuzzle of the head
until it flicks into flame.

His browning glory
a forest fire of one –
one with our rough places.

What the Woods Know

I call up my lover in the woods –
would he were here – and I tell
him about leaf-gold and everything bare
bearing him, borne away, and no sounds

but dogs' barks and bark sloughs
and bites of wind and a bitter
yellow fungus that looks unreal
and mushroomed troughs.

Trouw in Dutch means *marriage* and *true*.
It would be all those things,
cradled in a phone, cradled in an ear,
if he were not there, if he could be here.

Hearing him, I make a small turn in the gloaming,
heel resolute, the hang-up click.
But here he still is, in a shadow of birds
flying, slowly homing.

Bringing Up Baby
(*1938, Hepburn and Grant*)

Life is like that, running round a swamp
in search of a jaguar, or the crucial bone.
The jaguar's on the loose: it doesn't belong here.
See how it's doubled to its dangerous
and deadly carny brother, unrepentant
and marked out for destruction. Will they find
their pet, or get a fatal bite by moonlight?
See how, in the end, the jaguars usher us
to jail, for safety; trapped in vaudeville.

Life is like that; loons may be mistaken
for jaguars, and big game hunters miss their targets,
where men are prey, and Cary's – David's – frigid
fiancée, Miss Swallow, will not swallow.
Miss Hepburn's Susan refuses her obvious,
inborn lot. She'll smack those cocktail olives,
lift a car, and mock a moll, but still –
May Robson, dowager queen, so large with wealth,
steals every scene, so certain of her right.

A dog may bark to distraction, and bit by bit
un-dig a store of stolen boots, while Cary's
dressed in feathered robes or hunting gear,
his options clear. All seems to depend on finding
that intercostal clavicle, the *clou*,
of the dinosaur he'd re-assemble.
And yet, from ruined suits to broken glass
to shattered geese, there's nothing Auntie's
pot of gold – the magic grant – can't fix.

But Cary's still fixated on that dog,
he's trailing him *like Hamlet's ghost*, says Robson,
as if the simple link, the simple story
is only dog to bone, and how to fit
a dinosaur's old bones into their places.

Life is like that – Hepburn's swathe of chaos,
the heated hunt, and sliding into water
up to one's chin, by treacherous roots and moonlight.
They fall, and, rolling, smash up Cary's glasses.
It brings him close to her, if only to let
her see the true dark beauty of his eyes.
Kate will sway with delight until the whole
edifice of skeleton is rubble.

PERT EM HRU[1]

Gabriel Levin's *Coming Forth By Day*

PETER VERNON

BAUDELAIRE WANTED her painted out, Courbet complied, but Jeanne Duval is still triumphantly visible.

Jeanne Duval, Baudelaire's 'Black Venus', was banished from Courbet's 'The Artist's Studio' (1855), the subject of Gabriel Levin's title poem in this collection, but she may be regarded as emblematic of *Coming Forth By Day*: a black woman, unacceptable to polite society, painted out of history by white men. Jeanne is the opposite of a phenomenon, described by Daniel Arasse in *On n'y voit rien*, with regard to Gaspard, in Breugel's painting 'The Adoration of the Magi'. We are unable to see Gaspard; although he is there to be seen once he is pointed out, for his black face is painted against a black background. Despite the best efforts of Baudelaire and Courbet, with time, the over-painting has deteriorated and now we see Jeanne coming forth by day, from the penumbra into which she had been cast. The move from darkness into light is a touchstone of Courbet's work and Fritz Novotny reminds us that he 'showed a predilection for the old system of starting from the dark and working towards the light'.

Jeanne is a representative outcast in Levin's socially and politically engaged poetry, a commitment also to be found in his previous collections. In *Coming Forth By Day*, Marx provides the epigraph to 'Unveiled in Jerusalem', while in the title poem, we find Proudhon, Champfleury, Buchon, Cuennot and many other proto-socialists, rubbing shoulders with Courbet, in his '*L'allégorie réelle*', which is cited as epigraph to the poem. Meanwhile, in contrast to Jeanne, Courbet's naked muse or model emerges from one state to another, 'neither in / nor out of this world' as Levin writes. She has come forth by day, in an evident and explicit manner, while the painted-over Jeanne comes forth into day despite all efforts to paint her out of history.

'The Artist's Studio' is structured like a horizontal Anastasis (Christ's Harrowing of Limbo), which traditionally has a vertical structure with the damned below, and the saved above. In Courbet's painting, on the left are those who 'live on death', on the right are the artist's comrades, who 'live on life'; whilst in the centre, the artist with his naked muse or model, paints himself in the position of Christ: the creative artist as God, judging the symbolic figures in his painting: 'the whole world coming to me to be painted'. His is a supremely Romantic posture exemplified by his jutting beard and 'Assyrian profile' (Courbet's own description, cited by Levin). An Anastasis is a representation of judgement and Courbet's painting, seen in this way, is dynamic; it moves the reader in a continuous judgement, as the eye travels from left to right, reading the painting from the damned to the saved, with the central icon of Courbet himself, marking the transition and the judgement.

Since Levin's cosmopolitan existence has such bearing on his work, we might remind ourselves that he was born in France, received his education in America, and has lived in Israel for the last thirty years. Earlier works include four volumes of poetry: *Sleepers of Beulah* (1992), *Ostraca* (1999), *The Maltese Dreambook* (2008) and *To These Dark Steps* (2012), together with a number of translations from Hebrew, French and Arabic. In addition, he published a series of essays on the Levant, *The Dune's Twisted Edge* (2013). Entirely coherent with his subject matter and roots in the Mediterranean area, Levin's poetry expresses, implicitly and explicitly, an appeal for tolerance and understanding between peoples and cultures, and his themes include exile, wandering and transitions.

In the first collection, *Sleepers of Beulah* we find examples of exile when Levin packs Rimbaud off to Aden, writes of Ovid exiled on the Black Sea and records his own travels down the Nile in 'Aegypt', a sequence of nine poems. *Ostraca* continues his journeys through the Mediterranean, revealing his encyclopaedic knowledge, with translations from the different voices of Yehuda Halevi (twelfth-century Andalucia), the Christian pilgrim Egeria's travels in the Middle East in the fourth century: 'You who trudged into the arid interior,/ and out again, unruffled, though certainly humbled'. *Ostraca* also contains 'Rumi in the Hammam' based on the poetry of the Persian mystic, Rumi (1207–73). *The Maltese Dreambook*, continues the theme of wandering, giving us four voices exiled on Malta: Coleridge, Caravaggio, Abulafia and Levin's deceased friend Dennis Silk; his own exiled voice makes a fifth, who finds his alter ego in Abulafia who 'had fled from city to / city, and place to place'. While *To These Dark Steps* plunges the reader into war and rehearses the age-old biblical names of Sion, Ashkelon, Capurnum and Gaza together with the books and rites of Judaism and Islam – the Talmud, and Ramadan. 'I moved, like Ezekiel's wheels,' he writes, 'but my endorphins / must have kicked in, for I'm thinking in contraries'. With the figure of Ezekiel, Levin brings the war-torn locations and war-weary sides together, seen best in a poem called 'The Pity of War Distilled' which rehearses Shanfara's pre-Islamic 'Ode on the Letter L' in which Levin's Arab friend, Halileh finds himself: 'That's me, he exclaims, pointing to the open page: / the noble-hearted, adrift in this land, seeking/ refuge from insult and injury, drifts further afield'.

Levin's new collection, *Coming Forth by Day* is his most challenging so far. There are six sections, with most poems located in different areas of the Mediterranean: 'Across the Narrows' (Samos); 'Balthazar's Field' (Patmos); 'Unveiled in Jerusalem'; 'My Worn Pamphlets Closed Again On The Name Paphos' (the Lydian coastline); 'Coming Forth by Day'; and, finally, 'The Orphic

---

1   Transliteration of the hieroglyphs signifying 'Coming Forth by Day' (title page and p.56).

Egg'. The impermanence of the real, phenomenal world contrasted with the essence of things is perhaps more evident than in previous volumes; an idea made explicit in his version, in couplets, of a prose fragment from Numenius:

> From what lies plainly in sight we derive
> our notion of the body, and yet strive
> after the good no object sensible to the eye
> nor any single thing we might descry

The collection may be more challenging but Levin's voice is, unmistakeably, the same. It is an allusive voice pervaded with other writings and cultures where the words are given sound, and where space for breath is surrounded by silence between the broken and fragmented lines. As in earlier collections there is considerable focus on painting, music and poetry. However, the poetry here is a more lush, more daring, with more explosive effects – one could easily draw comparisons with the heightened rhetoric and alliteration of Lowell or early Heaney in lines like:

> (kew-kew – kew-wit!) I took for the spooked
> wryneck lashed to its spokes
> of song, and what might the polyps
>
>   sloshing against the shoreline,
> mistaken for IV bags,
> be telling me? ('Balthazar's Field')

Levin has always attended to stages of transition, in *Sleepers*, he wrote: 'It matters / we understand how all suffers change', and the chief transition of life is that into death, with the possible further transition of the soul into an afterlife. In 'Balthazar's Field', Levin translates an inscription dedicated to Bera, a priestess of Artemis, and asks:

> What did it mean to have a mind
> most faithful to cross over
> and return? (21)

Later in the same poem we find:

>   even so,
> at the bottom of mountains,
> living images surge
> in sudden disclosure, words
>
>   set down for the crossing
> and back.

However, this theme is even more significant in 'Coming Forth By Day' where Levin describes himself as neither 'in nor out of doors', sitting in a Paris Café, writing about writing a poem about Courbet who is in the process of painting 'The Artist's Studio':

>   as the draughtsman's tools
>
>   model the figure
> from the blank page,

> sitting, *leaning* on the table at the entrance,
>
>   neither out
> nor in (neither East nor West)
> dawn nor dusk, the book of what is
>   Manifested in Light,
> PERT EM HRU
> for the journey neither here
>   nor there –
> in transit, nor at rest –

The instant moment is captured when he amends 'sitting' to '*leaning*'. Images of transition are repeated as he imagines the voice of Courbet's muse or model speaking out of darkness, except for her 'naked, spell-/ bound self':

>   I sought refuge
> from the sun, and skies
>   to lose myself in – neither in
> nor out of this world,
>
> coming forth by day.

The title of the collection, *Coming Forth By Day*, is taken from *The Egyptian Book of the Dead*, a collection of spells whose purpose was to enable the soul to make all the necessary transitions and, after judgement, eventually to take its place in the Boat of Ra, and thus be enabled to travel through heaven in the state of *Akh* (blessed spirit of the dead, whose glyph is an ibis). The most complete example of these texts is a papyrus scroll, *The Book of Ani* in the British Museum. According to Vachel Lindsay, in *The Art of the Moving Picture*, the spells of judgement, transition and the medium of a scroll or reel are common both to Egyptian belief and film. Film, like Egyptian belief, involves judgement: 'The reel now before us is the mighty judgement roll dealing with the question of our departure' (Lindsay). In the poem 'The Artist's Studio' Levin develops an interpretation of the Judgement of the Soul, beyond the judgement of society that would one might expect from Courbet. Levin is evidently aware of the connection between dreams, transition of the soul and film since his vocabulary is frequently taken from film. In 'Balthazar's Field' he refers to 'countdown', 'blackout' 'spun-out footage' '*Finis*' 'shut-eye and shut down' and, speaking of the ass: 'I'd jump-cut / to Balthazar'. The title of this poem evidently owes something to Robert Bresson's film '*Au Hazard Balthazar*' (a Christian allegory in which Balthazar emerges as a saint): 'Balthazar I'll hazard / to crown later in the day'. While, in 'The Orphic Egg', he puns: 'in no time real as anything off the reel, advent/ or egress'.

In this volume, Levin concentrates on urgent creativity through writing and painting. We note a refusal to end-stop; the lines are enjambed, as though impelled by an overwhelming impetus in which nothing can be at rest; inspired by music he expresses a cauldron of ideas and connections:

>   sending out shoots, sudden, intervallic cross-
>   currents – what else might I toss
> in the mix? The musical idea you speak of alive
>   with the arcane, the hard drive

circuitry of technique I'd be at a loss

> to follow if the pieces didn't survive
> the talk

In Levin's poetry there is a constant tension between material evanascence and the permanence of art. In the extract above, we sense a struggle to find words for the music: 'what else might I toss / into the mix', but what is really significant is what lies beyond the sound of the music, it is the *idea* of the music, which enables him to reach back in his mind to connect to other works through: 'the hard drive / circuitry of technique'.

Levin focuses on the physicality of writing, employing a variety of images and juxtapositions. For example, he brings the reader close to the present of his own writing via an image of ancient Egypt: Thoth, the Egyptian scribe of the Gods, inventor of writing, 'rides the prow / of daylight'. (The same image is repeated later as Courbet rides on 'the prow / of his own ambition'). Thoth segues into Levin, now sitting at a Paris Café terrace:

> Thoth rides the prow
> of daylight – fashioner
> of the palette
> and ink-jar – and back
> to the marble-top
> table on which I've planted
> my elbows, fine-point Pilot,
> cahier, and sun-
> glasses

If Levin's subjects are consistent, then so too are his poetic techniques, many of which may be subsumed in the notion of the high seriousness and learning of modernism, being wittily undercut by the self-reflection of post-modernism. A notion well expressed by Greening: 'As dense an example of post-modern modernism as you will find.' The optimism, learning, and difficulty of modernism is preserved in Levin's poetry; but the ironies and self-reflection of post-modernism react with, and undercut, the high seriousness of modernism.

The idea is manifest when Levin juxtaposes high and low registers. For example, in 'Moonrise over Pythagorio', we are confronted with a 'goatshed' juxtaposed to 'Pentecostarion' while 'Balthazar's Field' opens with the banality of a snooze light, a clock falling off a nightstand, and the braying of an ass, which quickly shifts into 'the Thought that Dwells in the Light', Hölderlin's poem 'Patmos', *Les Très Riches Heures* and Greek inscriptions. Sparrows, their heads seen only, are 'on the hop' but then this is adjacent to 'wise to the world, / running through their own *Gnossiennes*', while street sounds become 'stochastic poetry of the carrefour'. The juxtaposition of registers functions to incarnate the sacred in the ordinary: the women cleaning on Patmos 'ajaxed/the windows of their faith'; one becomes 'Our Lady of Patience'. However, the divine is never seen in traditional pomp and glory, rather it is intuited, through the ordinary and banal, of which the ass Balthazar is a prime example.

Similar to the juxtaposition of registers is Levin's practice of taking a common idiom – 'punched your clock for good', 'the Almighty's a goner', 'touched in the head' – and wringing from these commonplaces additional significance. In 'Trône de David' he writes about a loquacious cabbie who: 'declaimed another poem, strictly for the birds'. He names the cabbie 'el Rawi' ('story teller', 'memorialist', 'poet'),[2] and as the poem develops, so the imagery increasingly climbs into the sacred. Thus 'for the birds', initially signifying 'undesirable', 'worthless', also connects to Levin's ornithological interests, and finally 'for the birds' hints to the flight of Ascension and the Paraclete. The sacred and the mundane are never far apart in Levin's work and in this poem they are brought together through the figure of his baby sister who becomes the model for a sculpture of the infant Christ: she may have a 'plug nose', but she is given the words of Christ on the cross: 'I thirst' (John, 19, 28). The living baby thus becomes transformed, by Levin's 'progenitor', the sculptor Marek Szwarc, who blows marble dust from his creation and, in 'bearing down' on the marble, gives birth to the figures of Virgin and Child:

> bearing down on the just
> dormant, the justly risen, until form
> uncoils under your blows, reforms,
> vaunts its own elisions: O tightly bound
> talismanic Angel of the Orient – lost, unsound
> hope, lift us in your armless embrace.

The line break after 'just' in the first line cited, forces the reader into readjustments of interpretation; nothing stays still, or is stable for long. Szwarc bears down on the just in the sense of 'the righteous', but this immediately becomes qualified as 'just / dormant', i.e. 'lightly sleeping', this then becomes further qualified as he reaches back to our original interpretation of righteous with 'justly risen', having connotations of the Resurrection.

A broken line in poetry or music allows space for the reader's eyes, ears and minds, and one of Levin's hallmarks is broken lines and gaps between lines, which can act mimetically: 'whose eyes plummet / into the gap words splinter'. Levin is explicit about the function: 'the gap that drills a hole in fore- / thought'; the broken lines and gaps leave space for breath, and space, within the poem, also acts to solicit, yet delay, creative interpretation:

> the quest
> launched in water and mud, in cryptic lore
>
> won't you tell us
>
> the score?

In these lines, the double space between 'won't you tell us' and 'the score' encourages the reader to look for ambiguity: won't you tell us what's going on / won't you count the rhythm of the musical score. Levin also draws attention to the gaps: 'rest your case in pulsing fissures / of subtones'. Breath and space are exemplified in broken

---

2 The name 'El Rawi' thus forges a connection with Pre-Islamic reciters of oral, tribal poetry such as Imru al-Qays, al Shanfara, and Hammad-al-Rawia, some of whom have been translated by Levin, most notably the *Mu'allaqa* by al Qays (*The Maltese Dreambook*, pp.53–8).

lines; however, it is the feet of the walker tramping regularly or irregularly which are echoed by the metrical feet of the poem. Levin gives a translation from 'Numenius ON THE GOOD' and in the following lines, the double gap, across the stanza, between 'breathe' and 'in' is a visual representation, encapsulating the act of *in*-spiration:

> embrace
> alone the good alone, where no living trace
> thrives, large or small, and rather breathe
>
> in unspeakable, wondrous solitude, a divine breeze

An 'inspiration' that leads to an ontological question, when he asks: 'what is Being?', at the end of the poem.

Levin uses pronouns to reach out and include the reader. When he adopts the voice of the 'gamin' portrayed in 'The Artist's Studio', he writes:

> I am the gamin on all fours, debatably
> touched in the head,
> trailing mud from out
> doors,
> [...]
> my line of vision – I too

have brought a charcoal
stick and convert
on foolscap
my elbows clamped to the floor

Levin gives the gamin voice and identity: 'I am the gamin', but at the same time he also identifies *with* the gamin as yet another artist figure, portrayed drawing on the floor to the right of the painter. 'I' in this poem could also be the viewer of Courbet's painting, and finally the reader is incorporated as the gamin breathing out addresses the reader/viewer: 'biting my lips / for your eyes alone'. Levin's pronouns are often determined late in the syntax, and therefore work is demanded from the reader: for example, in 'Coming Forth by Day', the subject of the opening lines 'he' and the speaker of the final section 'I' are unidentified – it is only upon re-reading that we can determine both refer to Courbet himself. After the first thirty lines of the opening section 'he confesses' which six lines later then segues into 'I shall plant / the peasant boy' at which point Courbet's identity is finally established. The delay in identity is part of the play, and since there are no notes, also forms part of Levin's generosity in assuming that we are as learned as he. Levin's ekphrasis of Courbet's painting is paralleled by his ekphrasis of Goehr's music, which I shall analyse in a subsequent paper.

from Third Nature

DREW MILNE

Rare Earths.

The irony of the plural rings bells, but rare earths are dug and then made. The ancient metres have spade, will mine, there be industry, and there be the brews, the pollution, sad waste and fake news for miners and smelters, not to mention sickness scars in the vicinity, and everything going all the way down to bacterial clouds and cancer clusters around the gene pool. The stumbling blocks are rich in hue and terror, but so fall the arms of sundry workers. Some of the industry will go on self soiling and some will go into administration, even if digital canaries get around to lighting up the screens of the trading floor. It's a shut case for birds of darkness, lungs of coal, and all about the margins, not the horizon or earth singular. Making losses is just this world's way of telling you to stop doing what you are doing. There are other relays, but losses are the undertakers. Sovereign among the bits of kit taken as read are guided missiles, laptops and smart phones, all firing away on scarce metals. Production dominance passed to China some years ago. Politicians sense opportunities amid human fodder digging for peanuts. Rare earths become geopolitical chips. There are bitter candles stored in the fridge under the nuclear bunker. The game of chicken is about supply chains and defence investment, but low prices take the laurels. Rare earths are not even rare, just diffuse. The back garden has its fair share, if not in sufficient concentration to make it worth the digging of the dirt. Not many seams are goers, or so illusion spawns make out and yet, in carrying on so, such spawns somehow find the patience to state that this is your life, your economics, your geology of value. Apply filters, and yes indeed, scarcer metals could be mined from plentiful but pricey aluminium wastes, or from zirconium production, mineral sands, tin, or fly ash, but not until yonder price points indicate significant margins. Military scrap would do the trick, though such recycling is a drain on battlefield resources. Neodymium driver magnets power up lightweight speakers. The strength of tetragonal crystal structures resists other attractions. Crystal lattices suggest obstinacy, strong enough to injure bodies caught in their clutches or falling out, lagging for a broken middle. Children have died swallowing the little bleeders. Floppy disks, credit cards and various masks have felt the pinch. Don't ask after the provenance or fate of batteries in hybrids. Solidarities shift the burden of production from one depletion to another. The Japanese are planning strategic autonomy from their ancient neighbours by digging cobalt-rich crusts in the deep sea. Your smart phone is not that clever. Some years down the line it will be easier to mine it for rare earths than dig it out of landfill.

It's the Flintstones, Stupid.

Names may be immaterial, just a soundbite of Adamic violence smeared thin over the lunar dirtscape. But names can stick, and do, even sticking patter to the landskip and undermining everything. Grime's Graves, a heath of heathen hue, groans under world heritage. Ideology is so mined in the interpretation centre. Grime is nevertheless a mask of Woden, maker of runes, wielder of wuldortanas or the twigs of glory. A mere kenning, but god of absolute slaughter and of wild hunts, the raven that feasts on human flesh, earthworker of darkness. Little is known and less is left to tell, it is all made up, even the cells and swords of elves, the dragons and sacrifice, not to mention timber temples, antimatter and the odd megalith. The tapestry of accommodation shows Woden as Odin and Wotan. Stains of the Roman romance wear their plagiarism lightly. Greek gods found themselves palmed off as cosa nostra before being mulched into the indifference of theological compost. Recycle, reuse and rewild. The Anglo-Saxons gambled on grave goods and gave us names for days, Wodenesday being our no deposit, no return, here's to the dark lord himself. Frigg, his quean, announces something for the weekend. Oh do be glued. Onwards to the sword and sandal remake. Axes turn to blades, reaping lands and woods on their way to being swept clear for crops and stone worship. Flint mines prefigure general depletion. The alleys through the mine-fields are sectioned off with plastic bunting and car strips that indicate how late rites of transport are stake-holders even over ancient tombs. Most deep pits are still too shallow really to shower the works with human allegories, however hard the urge troubles visitors and their symbolic capitals. Low galleries offer no head room. The sapphire miners of Madagascar would recognise kindred if anyone wanted to finance the trip. Shafts were dug, six men deep. Surface mounds speak of thousands of shifted tons. Red deer fed and clothed the miners, with left side antlers as picks of choice. One unproductive shaft was given over to a shrine, an altar with a chalk Venus, along with phallus and balls. The surrounds are a moonlit mecca for detectorists pitting their wits against the guards of heritage. By day, a single shaft is open to the public. Protective headgear is supplied. Children under ten are not allowed into the mine shaft and visitors are advised to wear sensible shoes.

Shifting Sands.

Aggregates and all the sand still to be counted for. Mere grains no longer, but grain upon grain, adding up to universal concrete. Water is the key ingredient, the conflict zone with deep pockets and slump tests to indicate performance parameters before the advent of subsequent metonyms. Sand can nevertheless be poured or born upon the wind, even run off as the rough side of polishing papers. Quartz, too, turns out to be handy for electrics, circuits and processors, and sheer building. From Cambodia to downtown skyscrapers, infrastructure projects crash over the dredged shore. Raw materials are only raw when seen from the other side of the cook-shop. Dredging barges do the development spread, as sands of crime run out over thin beds of reason. The appetite for construction builds artificial islands, black markets and PFI structure sumps. Supply is one thing, demand another, but the filling in the sandwich is a finite and depleted resource, what with all the blistered sands turning into artificial rock. 'Tis strange but true, skips of the daily dread, but Vietnam is running out of sand. Costs are rising as the bottom line fills the skies with concrete. Sand and gravel have become the world's most extracted materials, the majority commodities used up in human doings. Litter trays of construction. Sand scarcity beckons over the ruched horizon. Evening will dump truck the blue scale. CGI cannot offer filler for all. China has made more concrete in the last few years than the US in the last hundred. Low volatility environments condition the froth of financial services before being blown off by speculative corrections, corrections later rendered rational by retrospective fund managers. Asia watches sand spike on the market. Seasonal river beds are the new pits, and fish are fleeing declining waters. Keystone ingredients turn from child's play to rapid dwindling and then the languid tragedy becomes a made for cable special entitled the dissipation of the once and future commons. Cue sand mafias and gang wars for the right stuff. Sand is, even so, a special substance, such stuff and relations as lunar tides can take and wrestling scatter, and no cheap or mere matter for the grabber. Its former abundance is now all laid low among the erosions of the possible done over into done deals. Sand mining amplifies tidal waves, bringing the storm surge ever closer to downtown castles and the flooded sewers. The fine grain is coastal drift and shifting seas. The devil is in the filter.

Song of the Fatberg.

A team of eight hacked away with shovels for nine weeks, but the great fatberg in the sewers under Whitechapel, eight hundred feet long, and more than a hundred tons, was finally defeated. A London museum expressed interest in purchasing a section for its collection. It was on display in time for Xmas. Congealed fats are flushed down sinks and toilets before going on to bond with wipes, nappies and condoms. Sewer lard and sanitary detritus forms a stuff resembling concrete. Concerned parties spoke out against sewer abuse and engineers talked of declaring war. The fatberg leapt from obscurity to number one on the allegory parade. Wet wipes were in the frame. Like nappies, they seemed disposable, but were nearly indestructible. Almost none of the local restaurants had working fat traps. Fast food was clogging the arteries of the city. Even the rats could not digest the news. Despite the stench and fantastic consistency, fatbergs can, in part, be recycled as biogas. The air pollution is similar to natural gas, give or take the odd spillage of hydrogen sulphide. Any methane that isn't burnt becomes a lasting greenhouse gas. London's many psychogeographers were lost for words. The fatberg held out against gentrification until a sculptural installation appeared on the south bank, sponsored by a preventative health tech startup hoping to cash in on post-Xmas despair. Classical archaeologists declared that there was no evidence for anything comparable in the history of the Cloaca Maxima, whose outfall into the Tiber is still visible. Anthropologists were exploring the possibility that the fat-thin binary mapped the north–south axis, while fatbergs were discovered as far apart as Melbourne, Cardiff and Baltimore. Houses all over the capitalist economy make sacrifices to their very own household fatbergs. New builds promise green stucco. Sales of products for unblocking sinks, drains and toilets show year on year growth. The cocktails of biochemical cleaning agents pollute the water supply and many individuals unknowingly mix two different types of chemicals, with deadly results. The battle for the beach under the pavements is not over until the fatberg sings.

Concrete Poetry Again

Edwin Morgan

A Translator's Notebook (9)

edited by James McGonigal

In December 1964, shortly after his review of recent concrete poetry for *The Times Literary Supplement* of September 1964 (see 'A Translator's Notebook 8', *PN Review* 242), Edwin Morgan wrote a talk on the same topic for the BBC *Third Programme*. It would be produced by the poet George MacBeth and broadcast in June of the following year. The typescript in L/5 Box 2 of the Edwin Morgan Papers in Glasgow University Library is headed by a BBC disclaimer: 'not checked in talks department with "as broadcast" script'. And indeed the number of additional ideas and comments scribbled in its margins, mostly from Morgan but a couple from MacBeth, makes this draft even more interesting. I have included these as endnotes tagged to the original sentence, together with several editorial clarifications. Some of Morgan's glosses must relate to later presentations or seminars he gave on concrete poetry, extending the content of this talk, now illustrated by slides of the texts. We might say that the blend of literary and cultural criticism revealed here was itself a kind of 'translation', a rendering into the academic context of the time of avant-garde ideas that were too easily dismissible there. So this draft of a broadcast became part of the translator's notebook, to be revisited and extended during the years that followed. Material from these later talks is included here.

Concrete Poetry

The idea of a vanguard in literature has never had much acceptance in this country, though it's a commonplace on the Continent. The English Channel is a pretty narrow strip of water, but it's remarkable what an effective barrier it has been for the passage of ideas. The native argument is that this doesn't matter – that we prefer in our pragmatic way to get on with the job without worrying whether we're in the van or in the rear. There's a lot to be said for this attitude, but it can lead to a damaging kind of complacency. People may think that the poet is getting on with his self-imposed task, when in fact the absence of ideas and discussion may indicate lazy minds and smallness of spirit. Too many English poets since the Second World War have been busy stacking their neat little bundles of firewood, and have stopped planting trees. This is, in the overall cultural context, somewhat surprising, since it puts poetry so much out of step with the great changes that have been taking place in the other arts. The young painter or sculptor, for example, is working today in an atmosphere of marked creative excitement. This doesn't mean that the assemblages of Rauschenberg or the luminous pictures of John Healy represent the direction art has to take: it is simply that the artist feels himself to be in the midst of a varied and vigorous range of aesthetic activity. The English poet, on the other hand, has been contenting himself with a narrowed spectrum in which the traditional looms large and the exploratory has been almost forgotten.

The 1960s, however, have seen a tentative widening of the English poet's field of operations. Concrete or spatial poetry (both terms are used) is one of these extensions, and it's interesting that this at once links up with the spatialising tendencies already seen in the other arts. It's as if poets were suddenly becoming aware of a time-lag which had been withdrawing them further and further from the cultural experience of their fellow artists.

Concrete poetry is an international movement. It began about 1955 in Brazil and almost simultaneously in Switzerland. In Brazil, it was connected with the work of three poets, the brothers Augusto and Haroldo de Campos and Décio Pignatari; in Switzerland with the German-Swiss poet Eugen Gomringer. There was from the beginning contact between these poets, and this personal contact has been characteristic of the movement as it spread from country to country during the 1950s – mainly Germany, France, Netherlands, Italy, Czechoslovakia, Japan, and (about 1962) Britain and the United States. The movement now has a large body of work in many languages, a fair amount of critical theory behind it, and a growth and development from the original ideas into a variety of contiguous areas of experimentation. To mention a few of these areas: there is phonetic or phonic poetry, especially in France, in the work of Pierre Garnier and Henri Chopin, where the human voice, the spoken word, is used 'concretely' as a material and shaped electronically into new patterns and sequences of sound, rather as musical notes and natural sounds are re-shaped in concrete music.[1] There's the fold-in and cut-up composition techniques of Brion Gysin and William Burroughs. There's computer poetry, or the possibility of computer poetry. And finally there's kinetic art, and the possibility of involving concrete poetry in some situation or environment where physical movement is part of the aesthetic effect.[2]

But to go back to the beginnings. What was concrete poetry trying to do? Let me quote from the Brazilian manifesto, the 'Pilot-Plan for Concrete Poetry' (1958): 'Assuming that the historical cycle of verse as formal-rhythmical unit is closed, concrete poetry begins by being aware of *graphic space as structural agent*... Hence the importance of the ideogram concept, either in its general sense of spatial or visual syntax, or in its specific sense (as in Fenollosa and Ezra Pound) of a method of composition based on direct analogical comparison of elements.'

I think the main points are clear: the use of graphic space as a structural agent (the meaningful use of space as well as letters), so that the poem becomes a kind of ideogram, a sign, a concrete quasi-three-dimensional sign, a sign that exists as far as it can in space, i.e. even if it's only lying on the printed page it should give you a feeling, a consciousness of its spatial rather than its linear existence, so that you look at it as a whole, as a unit, rather than as something you read from beginning to end; and ideally of course the concrete poem will escape the page (which has all the tyranny of linearity associated with it as a habit that's very hard to shake off!) and become a sign in the world outside, whether engraved on glass, or cut in actual concrete either as a free-standing form or on the wall of a building, or (even better) if it becomes a neon sign in the darkness of a city at night, or is flashed for 10 seconds on a television screen.[3]

I think it is important here to notice the two polarities, as it were, of concrete poetry. On the one hand, this central concept of the spatial involves a search for systems of arrangement of the elements of the poem (which may be words or morphemes or even letters or numerals or marks of punctuation or typographical devices), and this search leads concrete poetry in the direction of the objective, the scientific, and especially the mathematical – i.e. you are often dealing with formulas of repetition or atomization of words, or permutations and combinations, or sets and series of progressive groupings, ungroupings and regroupings of words or parts of words; and this fits in with what the Brazilian group said in their manifesto, that they were 'against a poetry of expression' – the poet was not to be expressing his personality or individual experience so much as *doing something concretely with the material of the language.*

Well, that's one direction, or one aspect, of the movement. But on the other hand it's noticeable how often the concrete poets have emphasized the *function* of what they are doing within society.[4] Although the basis is not that of wanting to unite people in a warm emotional involvement, there's a strong desire *to get the poem out into society* if this can be done. The Brazilian poets were very politically conscious (as you'd expect in South America), and there are concrete poems about Cuba, about governmental oppression, about segregation and so on. They quote approvingly Mayakovsky's statement that, 'There is no revolutionary poetry without revolutionary form.' As an example of this sort of concrete poem, I'd like to read one of my own which I wrote about Sharpeville.[5] The

words are built on a grid of S and V, taken from the two parts of the name Sharpeville, and they're arranged in a pattern of alternating polysyllables and monosyllables meant to give a statement of dramatic opposition and menace.

starryveldt
slave
southvenus
serve
SHARPEVILLE
shove
shriekvolley
swerve
shootvillage
save
spoorvengeance
stave
spadevoice
starve
strikevault
strive
subvert
starve
smashverwoerd
strive
scattervoortrekker
starve
spadevow
strive
sunvast
starve
survive
strive
SO: VAEVICTIS

It's interesting that Eugen Gomringer the Swiss poet, a man who has written some of the purest and most non-political concrete poetry, has also reiterated the belief that concrete poetry has its function in society. I want to quote from his own manifesto,[6] where he says, 'We ought to conclude that the language of today must have certain things in common with poetry, and that they should sustain each other both in form and substance. In the course of daily life this relationship often passes unnoticed. Headlines, slogans, groups of sounds and letters give rise to forms which could be models for a new poetry just waiting to be taken up for meaningful use. The aim of the new poetry is to give poetry an organic function in society again, and in doing so to restate the position of poet in society. [...] *So the new poem is simple and can be perceived visually as a whole as well as in its parts. It becomes an object to be both seen and used: an object containing thought but made concrete* through play-activity, its concern is with brevity and conciseness.'[7]

A different defence of concrete poetry, but still within the general concern to produce objects for human use, comes from the Edinburgh poet Ian Hamilton Finlay, who wrote in 1963: 'One does not want a glittering perfection that forgets that the world is, after all, also to be made by man into his home. I should say [...] that concrete by its very limitations offers a tangible image of goodness and sanity; it is very far from the now-fashionable poetry of anguish and self [...] If I was asked "Why do you write concrete poetry?" I could truthfully answer "Because it is beautiful".'[8]

This emphasis which Finlay has on beauty suggests the strongly visual nature of much concrete poetry and also its closeness to art, to both painting and sculpture. Finlay is himself an artist and a toymaker. He takes great pains to have his poems printed exactly as he wants them, using different type-faces, coloured inks, special dimensions of page and so on. He has various Standing Poems which stand on the table like a piece of sculpture. He has kinetic poems where the action of turning over the page is a little reminiscent of the gradual unrolling of a Chinese horizontal scroll painting.[9] Some concrete poems by him and by other poets often seem to be like a certain kind of semi-abstract painting, and the words, unconnected syntactically but of course interrelated spatially and by juxtaposition, may suggest the colours and forms and even the tone and atmosphere of a picture. For example the French poet Pierre Garnier has a *Calendar* of twelve concrete poems describing or suggesting the months of the year.[10]

[At this point, Morgan reads 'Janvier' in French, saying: 'Although it's perhaps improper to read aloud a poem of this kind which depends on visual impact, I think its vibrance can be suggested by this method rather than through laborious description.' Spread across six columns, Garnier's poem is too spatial to reproduce here! – Editor]

Pierre Garnier has two rather interesting things to say about this visual poetry in an essay he published in 1965.[11] First of all, he calls it 'a poetry which is desensitized yet sensitizing'. That's to say, all the obvious appeals to sensuous reaction which might be elaborated through devices of diction and rhythm can be done away with, so that you have nothing but a collocation of individual words unrelated by syntax, and yet you have rising up from this a tingling chilly evocation of landscape and mood. Garnier is fond of talking of the poem as a 'centre of energy', a thing which by its construction, its articulation, is able to sensitize the mind of anyone who exposes himself to it. It's perhaps a little liske the practice of acupuncture in Chinese medicine: a Chinese doctor will undertake to cure your sciatica or migraine by inserting fine gold needles in carefully selected areas of your body – these needles are not connected to any electric or therapeutic apparatus, they cure you simply by being the right kind of needle placed in exactly the right spot, or so the Chinese say. In the same way, visual poetry depends upon an exact choice and placing of separate words which are not connected to phrases or sentences but which in spite of that carry a charge that you feel when you expose yourself to the grid of the whole poem. As Garnier says, 'What a difference there is between "The tiger is coming to drink at the river bank" and "T I G E R!".'

The second thing Garnier wrote in this essay was: 'Visual poetry is a happy poetry.' This links up with Ian Finlay's comment, you remember, that 'concrete poetry by its very limitations offers a tangible image of goodness and sanity... very far from the now-fashionable poetry of anguish and self!'

These statements, although they don't apply to all concrete poetry, are an important pointer to where this kind of poetry fits in. It is definitely post-existentialist, it's reacting against the world of Kafka and Eliot and Camus and Sartre. It's more likely to be interested in Yuri Gagarin than in Kafka. It looks forward with a certain confidence. It sees a probable coming together of art and science in ways that might benefit both. It takes *space* as a key-word, whether it's the uses now being made of space in poetry and art, or the actual exploration of

space that sets Gagarin as the Adam of a new era, or the revolution in our perception, in our way of looking at the world, which Marshall McLuhan described in his books *The Gutenberg Galaxy* and *Understanding Media* – the movement away from the printed book, away from the linear, towards the more 'open', instantaneous, spatial experience which technology has presented us with in newspaper and radio, film, television and advertising. I'd like to quote a couple of things McLuhan says (in a symposium *Explorations in Communication*, 1960). He's talking about the new media, which are usually referred to as media of communication. But, he says, 'All the new media, including the press, are art forms that have the power of imposing, like poetry, their own assumptions. The new media are not ways of relating us to the old "real" world: they *are* the real world, and they reshape what remains of the old world at will.'... This, I think, is relevant to concrete poetry. The concrete poem isn't meant to be something you would come across as you turned the pages of a book. Most concrete poems still are, but that is not ideal. It would rather be an object that you passed every day on your way to work, to school or factory or office, it would be in life, in space, concretely *there*.[12] ... And then again, McLuhan says, talking about Russian achievements in space technology, rocket engineering and so on, not being matched by applications of technology to culture, for example, in television, newspaper and magazine layout, advertising techniques and industrial design... And he says: 'The Russians are impotent to shape technological *culture* because of their inwardness and grimness. The future masters of technology will have to be *lighthearted*: the machine easily masters the grim.' – At first sight this is a curious statement, but it fits into the context of the new mood I've tried to describe, the mood *against* grimness and inwardness and angst and *for* what Garnier calls happiness, what Finlay calls beauty, what Gomringer calls play.

These words *happiness*, *beauty*, *play* are all a bit suspect today. We find ourselves asking doubtfully whether we ought to take with any seriousness an art form which has this sort of basis. But such opposition should probably warn us that concrete poetry is on to something. I think most people would find if they gave it a chance that there would be a point at which they did take it seriously. Such a point might be Pierre Garnier's *Calendar*, where certain obviously evocative effects are produced as well as a concrete pattern which forces us to look at the individual words as if we were seeing them for the very first time. Or it might be a beautiful piece of imitative form like Ian Finlay's poem 'This is the little burn that plays its mouth organ by the mill', where the winding course of the stream and the sound it makes are simultaneously suggested by a trail of Ms in different type-fonts and colours of ink. Or it might be an idea which is given brief compressed complex existence in concrete form, as in Dom Sylvester Houédard's 'Christmas Poem 1964' in which the two words *sol* and *thalamus* (standing for 'sun' and 'bride-chamber' in a religious context) are made to interpenetrate step by step in a movement from east to west.

I would like to finish by reading three concrete poems of different types, which will perhaps help to define the areas of value which this kind of poetry is attempting to explore.[13]

The first is a short untitled poem by Eugen Gomringer. This represents the 'purest' sort of concrete, with emphasis on the separated word. It's a poem about qualities and relations, about what relations are possible and what not, about what relations are natural and what relations only exist in art. It begins with the most easy relationship and moves out into those that tease the mind and make it think and wonder:

from deep
to deep
from near
to near
from grey
to grey
from deep
to near
from near
to grey
from grey
to deep

from two
to four
from three
to one
from one
to four

from deep
to two
from four
to near
from grey
to one[14]

The second poem is one of my own called 'Pomander'. The
lines are arranged in the imitative form of a pomander, but
that is not the main thing. I take the idea of the pomander as
a round object which is opened up to release its fragrance – I
had one in mind particularly which opened like the segments
of a cut orange. I use this to bring out the theme of opening
up the poem, of 'exploding' it spatially, and in a broader sense
of opening out life, life itself (or the world) as a pomander, its
secrets and treasures and rare things not to be hoarded but
opened up and made available. To keep this wide-ranging
theme viable within a concrete form, the poem uses associat-
ed imagery within a narrow range of soundeffects:

POMANDER

pomander
open pomander
open poem and her
open poem and him
open poem and hymn
hymn and hymen leander
high man pen meander
o pen poem me and her
pen me poem me and him
om mane padme hum
pad me home panda hand
open up o holy panhandler
ample panda pen or bamboo pond
ponder a bony poem pomander opener
open banned peon penman hum and banter
open hymn and pompom band and panda hamper
o i am a pen open man or happener
i am open manner happener

happy are we open
poem and a pom
poem and a panda
poem and aplomb[15]

And the last poem is an untitled piece by the American poet
Robert Lax. It conveys very well, I think, the consciousness
of space which pervades this poetry as it will more and more
pervade our lives:

the port
was longing

the port
was longing

not for
this ship

not for
that ship

not for
this ship

not for
that ship

the port
was longing

the port
was longing

not for
this sea

not for
that sea

the port
was longing

not for
this &

not for
that

not for
this &

not for
that

the port
was longing

not for
this &

not for
that[16]

Various relevant texts are collected fore and aft of this script in the file. There is a quote from the Journals of Gerard Manley Hopkins: 'All the world is full of inscape, & chance left free to act falls into an order as well as purpose.' Morgan's underlining ignores the teleology of faith but underscores the aesthetic openings to be found in aleatory and other formal experimentation. There is a useful bibliographical chronology of concrete, from the letter to the *Times Literary Supplement* of 25 May 1962 from the Portuguese poet E. M. de Melo e Castro to later articles by Bob Cobbing and Dom Sylvester Houédard dated 1971, 1974 and 1977. There is also a new Introduction to the talk, referring to the public and open-air exhibition of concrete poetry, including Morgan's own, at the 1967 Brighton Arts Festival and to recent books by Stephen Bann and Emmett Williams. This Introduction and the marginal glosses within the BBC talk suggest that he made use of the script's content in a variety of later talks. These he would often illustrate with slides of the poems under discussion, so that the visual dimensions were opened up. And his running commentaries on particular poems are also preserved in the file, giving a closer sense to his speaking voice than the slightly more formal BBC *Third Programme* context. Here are two examples, related to poems he read in the broadcast:

From deep: Purer still! Gomringer's more recent work, more abstract here: a poem about qualities & relations. He wants you to think about what kinds of relation are possible and what are not – from deep to deep yes it begins plain sailing – from near to grey – perhaps from deep to near – yes... & so on until the poem reaches its turn, its pivotal point – it moves off into feeling of another dimension – It reminds me of Arthur Koestler's bisociation theory – two separate fields of thought suddenly intersecting with a shock – what is the relation between the word deep and the word two??

Pomander: Imitative form, but that's not the main thing. Point about pomander – a round object that you have to open up to release its fragrance – it opens like segments of an orange. I want this to bring out the theme of opening out the poem, of exploding it spatially, & in a broader sense the theme of opening out life, life itself as a pomander, secrets and treasures and rare things not to be hoarded but opened up and made available, hence the Buddhist hymn om mane padme hum the jewel in the lotus – open up the lotus with its petals like segments of the pomander & and let men see the jewel – open up the panda hamper and let the panda out – the panda follows on from the Indian/Tibetan references. Open up life for poor or the oppressed – banned peon penman – perhaps South American poets and their difficulties. And so on. And this is all done within a deliberately restricted range of letters as you can see – words all connected by sound – to give impression of this round object.

In his practice and analysis of 1960s concrete poetry, then, Morgan reveals the transformation in his own emotional and creative life at this time. He would end such illustrated talks along the following lines, also on file:

These examples will give you some idea of what the concrete poets have been doing. I would be inclined myself to discount some of the more extreme claims which are made for concrete (especially in Germany), but on the other hand I am quite sure that it is on to something important and worth watching. The battle between linearity and spatiality which concrete reflects is something that is in life itself & is going to have far-ranging consequences. Two simple practical illustrations: (i) when you enter a very modern newly-designed shop or a large open-plan house you may (especially if of the older generation) have feelings of unease, you don't see the familiar signposts & and you don't quite know where to go or what to do – this is because the concept of space has taken over & it needs some adjustment on your part. (ii) Recent agitation in universities for seminars as against lectures – there are no doubt various reasons for this, but the underlying and probably unsuspected reason is that the lecture is linear and the seminar is spatial & the younger generation senses this and wants the spatial! The problem of concrete, then, is not hard to relate, if you start to think about it, to changes that are going on in our society. And if it is important that the arts should be sensitive to these movements of thought and movements of perception which affect or are going to affect people's lives, & I certainly think this is part of their function, then concrete poetry has its place. What it gives us is something quite small, but it may be a small key that opens a large door.[17]

MORGAN'S NOTES & COMMENTS

1 Cf. also concrete art (Max Bill). Ernst Jandl, Bob Cobbings – sound poems, non-electronic.
2 GMcB suggests: 'Simpler not here perhaps?'
3 Cf. McLuhan, *The Medium is the Message*, p. 123.
4 Some is humorous, some is satirical, some is religious/meditational.
5 JMcG: Sharpeville was a black township south of Johannesburg where, on 21 March 1960, security forces fired on a crowd demonstrating against apartheid laws, killing 67 and wounding about 180. The final line of the poem means 'Woe to the conquered', with perhaps a glance forward towards another ultimate victory.
6 In *Augenblick* No. 2, Baden-Baden, 1954; transl. in *Image*, Cambridge, 1964.
7 Cf. his motto in *Konstellationen* (1962): 'It is interesting to observe that as technical applications have increased in complexity [...] languages have increased in simplicity, until today we are considering the ultimate compression of information in the simplest possible forms' Cf. post-war development of electronic computers (EM!).
8 Written to Pierre Garnier, 17-2-1963, quoted in *Image*, as above.
9 e.g. Autumn Poem, Canal Game.
10 In *Les Lettres* No. 30.
11 In *Les Lettres* No. 30.
12 Does this mean it's moving away from 'poetry' or 'literature' as we know it? A difficult question which you may want to raise later in discussion. It's true that some of the best-known concrete poets are not primarily poets – they may be architects or linguists or artists – BUT still the medium is words – It may be a parallel development to poetry – cf. other arts overflowing borders today. Quote Bann Intro p. 27.
14 GMcB suggests: 'Perhaps worth stressing again that the e.g.s you can read aloud restrict your choice?' Thus E.M. adds: I would emphasize however that most concrete poetry is for the eye rather than the ear, and the number of examples which can be read aloud is relatively small.
15 Edwin Morgan, *Collected Translations* (1996) p. 294.
16 Edwin Morgan, *Collected Poems* (1996) p. 173.
17 In *Poor. Old. Tired. Horse.* No. 10, Edinburgh, 1964.

Making Sense

Don Paterson, *The Poem: Lyric, Sign, Metre* (Faber) £25

Reviewed by HAL COASE

When giving your evidence, begin at the beginning and go on till you come to the end: then stop. This does *sound* like the definition of straightforward, no-nonsense, honest reasoning. To set out an argument from first principles is nonetheless a hell of a tricky thing to do not least because, unless you do happen to be a professional solipsist (which may yet be one broadly held definition of 'a poet'), you must always be aware that the end of your logic is the beginning of someone else's inquiry. To put it another way: beginnings and first principles, at least where poetry is concerned, are difficult to agree on.

Don Paterson's *The Poem*, a mammoth work best read without any hope of ending it, is both a simple cry for poetics to go back to first principles and a pretty thorough demonstration of why this is never as simple as it sounds. To begin with Paterson's beginning: the ur-form of poetry was 'easily memorisable speech' and it's ability to store vital information would, in primitive societies, have seen it acquire 'a reputation as a mantic art'. Poetry, it follows, is 'a naturally occurring mode of human speech' produced under two pressures: 'emotional urgency and temporal constraint', which, the conclusion states, 'discloses' to us 'the underlying unity' of the material world.

To recognise the mnemonic, the emotive, the spontaneous and above all the natural origins of whatever might've once been *poetry* is a fairly anodyne stance. To suggest that these qualities must therefore be the frames of reference with which we can analyse *the poem* in English in the twenty-first century is a different matter altogether. The former is a wholly descriptive stance, the latter a potentially prescriptive one.

This might sound like a difference of degree, a question of how and when to use differing interpretative frames, but to see the broadest beginning (speculations on the origins of poetry) from the vantage of a narrow end (a defence of what, unhelpfully but for the sake of ease, might be called 'mainstream' lyric poems in English from the last two-hundred years) is to project backwards from subjective conclusions, to flow from delta to spring, in a move that's not only totalising but also counterproductive. You could, if you were so inclined, just as easily tell the story of ur-poetry as a privileging of a sibyllic, intellectual and strikingly methodical mode of communication reliant upon artifice (Veronica Forrest-Thomson's *Poetic Artifice* works, I'd say, on similar suppositions). In either case, such a story had better be the bitter end of significant argumentation not its starting point.

To be clear, the three essays that make up the book are, unlike the first's opening chapter, in no way preoccupied with a history of poetry in this wider sense and I want to get past Paterson's beginning. But the book's weakest parts are those where a particular intervention into contemporary poetic practice, reception and criticism makes a claim to the universal. Which is to say that this book feels necessary and long overdue; it is by (occasionally handbrake) turns imprecise and pernickety; it is full of such a passion for disentangling poetics from pseudo-philosophies that it can't help but get itself tangled up in other strands of thought (structural linguistics, neuroscience and free jazz: entanglers-in-chief); it is perhaps without parallel in recent times as an *ars poetica* which entirely deserves that name (with all its heritage and haughtiness); and I only wish it didn't occasionally fall back on atavistic rationalisations for an otherwise level-headed defence of the 'middle-ground' of poetry today.

This defence is carried out across all three essays through an appeal to the necessity of formal balance so that moments of imbalance may be properly felt (this makes enough sense, although why, I kept thinking, we should expect to agree on where the *centre-point* of such a balance should be placed is more difficult to explain).

The first essay, 'Lyric', is concerned with the balance between sound and sense. There are the predictable scuffles with the 'avant-garde' and modernist maxims (the rest of the book is largely free of this), even if Paterson sometimes arrives at similar positions from his own path. I remain completely unconvinced of the 'iconicity' of words ('*words sound like the things they mean*... through a deep rule of synaesthetic representation') and at times felt that this stage of the argument ran counter to a much more persuasive account of connotation and its significance.

The second essay, 'Sign', explores the function of tropes within a poem and, most productively, the complex balance between abstracts and concretes. Its boundless ambition is matched only by its capacity for neologising ('formeme', 'aeteme', 'patheme', 'aseme'). The problem here is Paterson's largely unspoken belief that a poem always seeks to form 'an unusually unified' speech act, even whilst offhandedly acknowledging with a footnote that 'there are poetries [...] where "unified statement" is not automatically assumed to be the poem's ambition. Horses for courses.' Horses for courses, indeed.

The third essay, 'Metre', is a byzantine attempt to arrive at a new method of scansion that can properly balance speech-strong and metre-strong readings. It is not, refreshingly, another run-down of metrical techniques and their 'appropriate' use. Instead, it starts from scratch with the notion of 'pulse' (as with Eliot, Henri Bergson never feels far away) and goes on to exhaustively classify the different pressures exerted on poetic rhythm.

The difficulties here emerge once Paterson has more or less convincingly rejected the overbearing emphasis that most prosodic accounts give to metre. The aim is to replace metre-strong scansion with a sensitive combination of metrical template, lexical stress, phrasal stress and 'sense stress' (e.g. '*Where* do you think you're going?': an angry parent; 'Where do you *think* you're going?': a person with a map helping someone completely lost).

But this inevitably leads, as Paterson readily acknowledges, to a heavily subjective method of scansion that can have no final say. The essay remains stronger than the other two as a result of this direct acknowledgement of its own indeterminacy. If it's in danger, as Paterson puts it, of moving past 'a threshold beyond which one is becoming impractically remote from the aims of the exercise', this could have been resolved by a plainer and lengthier interpretation of the relationship between Paterson's prosodic 'contours' and how meaning is constructed.

To return at the end to the beginning, I don't doubt for a second that Paterson takes his view of poetry's pre-historic function as contiguous with his linguistic and metrical analyses nor that bold claims that take us to the extremities of thought are in some way always needed to keep us focssed on the drudgework of detail. But throughout *The Poem* I was struck by the sense of an argumentative link gone AWOL, an unstable gap between the minutiae at the centre of Paterson's readings and the reach of his claims, not helped by a curt conclusion that makes no attempt to pull these two proceedings together. Shelley's caricature of Wordsworth in 'Peter Bell the Third', a blast of angry adoration, is about as close as I can get to this: 'He had a mind somehow / at once circumference and centre.' Here the phrase might read as coolly glib but it's worth remembering that Shelley later used it to describe all poetry's claim to knowledge. When you're dealing with the centre and circumference at once, in the moment they seem to *collide*, you're thinking about poetry.

Coming to Grips

Kazim Ali, *Inquisition* (Wesleyan University Press) £11.29;
Brenda Hillman, *Extra Hidden Life, among the days* (Wesleyan University Press) £23

Reviewed by JOE CARRICK-VARTY

Kazim Ali's *Inquisition* is a fearless pursuit of thinking even to the point of disassembling the brain itself. The poems seek their own impossible origins; they find brave and surprising forms to map the journey.

'John', a poem typical of this quest, is structured with a series of coordinates; a trail for the speaker who is lost and looking for a way (all the way) back: 'Who was I when I was writing this name'. Ali starts small (molecularly small), 'Copper oxidizes to green', then pans out, following with meticulous attention as oxygen becomes first a part of air, then breath, then life: 'Air packs itself tight in the seed / Seed unspools in the ground writing the biography of dirt' (Can I just say: the biography of dirt! Written by a seed!). A lovely image concludes the journey: 'A little further down the road another tower is going up'. The subtle proximity of 'down the road' gives the line a compelling relatability, while the blasé 'going up' jars for all the right reasons: a thing as huge as a tower goes nowhere, really, but neither do pine trees or mountains. The trick is Ali shows us the going. Because everything was tiny once.

Many of my favourite poems in *Inquisition* deploy single-line stanzas in an attempt to manage this deft oscillation of perspective, each stanza representing a stage, a stepping stone, and each piece of white space representing the shift into a new context. The form is doing something clever here. While the poems are largely unpunctuated they are not without structure. As in 'The Failure of Navigation in the Valley', a thought will often break mid-line, mid-phrase and begin talking to itself: 'Unseen I wander through the thorny place of what I no that ain't it'. This layering of voice is one of the collection's achievements, and its effect is an unresolved kind of snappiness, a continuation, a searching for: 'In the mountains I have no GPS I don't know where to go'. The poems are comfortably lost, comfortably 'going' (there we go again) somewhere, be that place a lighthouse or a yoga class or home: 'Who am I where is my home who will be there to let me in'. When the voices interject you listen, you join in the conversation, you become a part of the journey. Which leads me back to the form (and its bravery). These are not just poems, they are thinking in action, a brain rendered readable on the page; deciding and arguing and hoping and loving: 'Who will I be next and in that life will you know me'.

Brenda Hillman's *Extra Hidden Life, among the days* is another kind of brain on the page: the brain of a forest; its web of roots underground; 'the world above and below'. Accompanied by a collage of photos, Hillman creates an ecosystem out of glimpses and glimmers that are haunting in the way they reach (and reach) for a finale that never comes. The poems bleed between one and other, often ending with dashes or ellipses; 'such a small word, *time* / yet it is friends / with both nothings–' and it is this unending quality that makes the book so unavoidably looming (especially in the face of climate change). Yes, you will carry these poems around with you. And they will pop up when you least expect it.

One need just skim the contents page to glean Hillman's ecological imperative. Titles such as 'Species Prepare to Live After Money', 'As a Sentence Leaves its Breath', 'So, Bacteria Also Have Their Thunder', make no bones about their post-human vision, one that finds the speaker firmly rooted in the liminal: 'standing at the edge of / some low scrub of hills as if / humans were extra or already gone'.

So, a brain of the forest, one consciousness, #savethetrees and all that: you're thinking preachy? Didactic? Annoying (maybe)? Wrong. Hillman takes the phrase Climate Change Poetry (what a horrible phrase) and buries it. You'll find nothing forced. No moral 'takeaway' or damning indictment. More important for Hillman is the texture of her forest; the depth of her soundscape; 'The visible is thick but the invisible is thicker.'

Whether it's the sound (and sibilance) of light melting through a canopy: 'species with names the tree / can hold in the shale shade brought / by the ambulance of art', or a bleakly original way of describing moonlight: 'that raw moon / slashes your bed/through the cage of the blinds' (Didn't you hear? The moon can slash now), or an idea transfiguring and transforming (I'm thinking particularly of 'On a Day, In the World' when 'the willing / burden of an old belief' becomes 'the color time / will be when we are gone'), the poems sing as if alive, and they sing loud enough for a you-shaped-fold to open in the page and close forever: 'Otters swam in the lagoon, / the gates opened in the reeds... Far out to sea 10,000 whales/swam'.

Re-verse

Various

Reviews by YOGESH PATEL

'You shouldn't be here'
Mona Dash, *A Certain Way*
(Skylark Publications)

You strolled into a British pub in a sari
With that Moon shouting boldly from the forehead
No wonder the Indian lion roars at the Brexit lock
As the lager louts gurgle *You shouldn't be here*
But in that suitcase full of roars you sing your way
Protect and hold gently that love your guiding light
You shouldn't be here but you're here to walk the walk
Like a bride now to cross the threshold *A Certain Way*

*

'A Dastidarian Construct'
Rishi Dastidar, *Ticker-Tape*
(Nine Arches Press)

In the Matchstick Empire waving ribbons of sentences
Attached to the capitalism or Londonistan
A poet points a giant fan to blow them
Down below the zone six

Not up in the air for the dignity
After all no poets should be standing
Off the table holding the pint in one hand
They should be on the table shouting liberalism
Amen to *shirshasana*
But the Dastidarian construct is a dream
For being braver asleep than awake
Amen to page 69
There is no page 96

*

'A Homing Quest'
Bashabi Fraser, *The Homing Bird*
(Indigo Dreams Publishing)

Hate is not liquid
Time is, and yes, the culture is
Therefore flows the water free
Between and under
The Howrah Bridge
And the Dean Bridge
Bridging the tale of two cities
A poet standing and wondering
Ah, 'the sky between us two skies
This border born of blood split free
Makes you my friend, my enemy.'
With 'blushing bridehood'
That floods both cities...

Debts to the Dead

Nausheen Eusuf, *Not Elegy, But Eros* (NYQ) $15.95; Sheryl St Germain, *The Small Door of Your Death* (Autumn House) $17.95

Reviewed by REBECCA FOSTER

Poetry can be a way of approaching the unbearable, of taming a loss and giving it aesthetic shape. Two recent collections adapt the time-honoured forms of elegies and prayers as they ask what we owe to the dead.

Nausheen Eusuf is a Bangladeshi poet currently studying for a PhD at Boston University. The title of her debut collection, *Not Elegy, But Eros*, playfully denies the very structure it so often employs. The table of contents is in fact rife with elegies, as well as prayers and odes, but these traditional modes function not as a constraint but as a starting point for richly alliterative and allusive verse that contrasts Bangladesh and America while paying homage to departed family members and those lost to violence and disaster.

The narrator's dead parents, sometimes addressed directly in the second person, are a ghostly presence pervading the book. The multi-part poem 'Ubi Sunt', calling to mind a recurring motif from elegiac poetry, asks 'Where are they now?' three times. 'Prayer to My Father' laments the former engineer's dementia and physical deterioration – 'Your own infrastructure in disarray' – and repeatedly begs for forgiveness in lines that liken the father to the deity: 'Forgive us, father, for the indignity / of the catheter'. In 'Musée des Beaux Morts', a tip of the hat to W. H. Auden, the narrator gives a tour of her late parents' artefact-filled house – textbooks, wedding photos, knick-knacks. The plush descriptions cease with a jolt in the final stanza as she sums up: 'Well, there you have it, folks, the crap / one collects over a lifetime'.

Allusions range from Charles Baudelaire to Oscar Wilde, while epiphanies arise during everything from watching Alfred Hitchcock's *Psycho* to observing crab behaviour on the Massachusetts coast. Eusuf effectively switches between everyday and exotic metaphors: 'ill-stacked Tupperware' symbolises mental disorder, while the guarded beloved is a pangolin to be disarmed by love and attention. Although there are occasional end rhymes, as well as internal rhymes and homophones, most often the sonic resonance comes from alliteration, as in 'the bright blooming of umbrellas / bobbing gently through the drizzle' and 'the dust of desuetude settling like a dog at your feet.' 'Ode to the Slow Life' embodies its languid advice with lots of alliteration, sibilance in particular.

Personal losses later cede to tragedy on a wider scale, with tributes written for the victims of a garment factory collapse and those killed in political violence and terrorist attacks in Bangladesh. The title piece is in memory of Xulhaz Mannan, an LGBT activist murdered in 2016, who is presented as a willing martyr for the cause of equality: 'I have lain down among the rushes and offered myself... I have faced the flash of steel, the howl / of unholy voices.' Other poems discuss depression and the struggle to belong in America. But it isn't all heavy material; Part V is particularly light-hearted, what with the wordplay in 'Ding an Sich' and 'The Overall' and the relentless end rhymes in 'Ode to the Joke'.

The Small Door of Your Death, Sheryl St Germain's seventh collection, is in memory of her son Gray, who died of a drug overdose in 2014, aged thirty. The director of the MFA program in Creative Writing at Chatham University and co-founder of the Words Without Walls project, St Germain turns her family history of alcohol and drug use into a touchpoint. In multiple poems named after a suit of tarot cards – 'Three of Swords', 'Ace of Swords' and so on – she portrays her family line as reckless and self-destructive. The first in this series, 'Suit of Swords', alternates between unsettling internal slant rhymes (paddling, peddle, settle) and soothing sibilance ('I stroke him to sleep, singing some song / about summertime') to reflect the family's volatile mixture of danger and love.

Later on the poet uses the metaphor of a flood to describe alcoholism rising up through the generations of the family. Overpowering natural forces are evoked to underline how futile it is to try to control a loved one's drug habit. In 'Loving an Addict', the turbulence of the relationship with her son, sometimes maddening and other times tender, is like 'troubled' skies assailed by 'gusts' versus 'the kiss of a breeze'. Spruce and pine needles remind her of the needles Gray would use to shoot up; the title phrase refers to the puncture on the back of his hand that delivered a fatal dose of dope.

Like Eusuf, St Germain incorporates the very forms she claims not to value. She ends the book with a prayer for her son, having earlier found herself lighting a candle in a church by a statue of Mary – 'I don't believe, but here I am... // She lost a son too.' In 'Versions of Heaven' she recalls golden moments from their relationship – dancing to R.E.M., a road trip through Iowa, and watching Gray perform with his band – and wistfully imagines him 'playing songs for saints'. Also like Eusuf, St Germain frequently uses the second person, usually to address her son, though sometimes also of herself, to distance herself from loss.

The book moves beyond its melancholy subject matter in Part 5, which opens with poems set in France and the Netherlands six months after Gray's death. 'Reasons to Live: The Color Red', one of the overall standouts, affirms life's sensual pleasures – everything from the smell of brand-new cowboy boots to luscious fruits. In 'At the Keukenhof', a walk through a field of vividly coloured tulips makes her think of her son's zest for life: 'He who loved intensity over almost anything, / would have felt it in these flowers.'

These two excellent collections travel across generations and continents to trace family legacies and look for simple joys to outstrip the litany of bad news. Employing similar sonic techniques and a multi-part structure that moves from sombre into lighter material, they suggest that the writing of poetry itself might be a ladder out of the depths of grief.

From the Archive

Issue 143, January–February 2002

JANE YEH

From a contribution of seven poems alongisde 'Convent at Haarlem' and 'Self-Portrait after Vermeer'. Fellow contributors to this issue include Grevel Lindop, Michael Hamburger, Mimi Khalvati, Christopher Middleton and John Gallas.

VESUVIUS (IN THE PRIESTS' QUARTERS)

When it came, we were getting ready
For bed. The gowns lay on the mattresses,
White as palms open for a coin.

I always loved how they spread themselves,
Armless & headless, across the sheets,
Loved that perfect stillness of things

Dropped from a great height. They stretched
The length of the beds like so many
Paper dolls. That night

The sandals waited on the floor, soft
Brown mouths, open & dumb as those
Of children. I loved how the feet

Came down with a slap, the straps
An embrace. We were kneeling
When it hit. [...]

Nox est perpetua

Toby Martinez de las Rivas, *Black Sun* (Faber & Faber) £9.90

Reviewed by ANDREW FRAYN

In his second collection, *Black Sun*, Toby Martinez de las Rivas develops and strengthens his poetic voice. He moves from the introspection of early verse to mature reflection on the state of the world; the self-apostrophising *Tobe* is less prominent. The volume is highly formal, strikingly exploring the possibilities of the sonnet: the two poems not obviously in that form, opening the first and final sections, combine their octave and sestet to achieve a structural unity. The themes he addresses remain consistent from earlier work, the materiality of the text and body allied with the tension between faith and despair; recent world events lurk just out of sight. The 'black sun' motif appears in his earlier collection, *Terror* (2014). The first stanza of its first poem, 'Twenty-One Prayers for Weak or Fabulous Things' ends: 'I speak this prayer into the black sun'. A dislike for conventional publishing ornaments led to the solid black circle that separates its sections, and that disc returns in *Black Sun* at five times the size, now a focal point. These verses return to eschatology, as in 'The Same Night Waits for Everyone', and in the back matter the same black circle obscures the repeated word 'Judgement'. Martinez de las Rivas refuses closure, however, with a white sun on the black facing page.

A key aspect of the developing force of Martinez de las Rivas's voice is his determination to stand apart. 'England' opens the middle section, suggesting its centrality to his identity. However, there is no nostalgia: 'the bailiff parks up with his sandwich / & the burnt-out car is mercifully at rest'. The Petrarchan sonnet is reversed, turning to a closing octave at '*Hermosa*', the Spanish word evoking a beauty that battles with the death throes of heavy industry. He wrestles with his Anglo-Hispanic national identity, notably in 'House of Blood', where he connects personal responsibility and international conflict via the esoteric, Eliotesque endnotes tell us, the responsibility of his antecedents for building ships sunk at war.

The English tradition of religious poetry echoes through *Black Sun*. In the opening poem, 'i.m. J.F. 1978–2006, & to O.H.', modernity creeps into a pastoral that recalls Robert Herrick, a girl roused from texting among more conventional symbols of spring. 'Hunting Kestrel, Danebury' evokes Gerard Manley Hopkins in its swooping, rising and falling rhythms, while 'At Lullington Church/To My Daughter' intertextually invokes the Corpus Christi Carol, its refrain echoing the church's name while scaling up the original: 'The falcon has flown away with history'. Historical change is mapped onto the body as Martinez de las Rivas worries about both his own aging and the wider legacies left for future generations.

The difficulty of hope in the twenty-first century is a recurring concern, particularly prominent in the final section '*resurrection of the state*'. A trio of diptychs plays with the nature of allegory and encoding, offering parallel meditations on time's vastness and how we fill it. Martinez de las Rivas draws powerful parallels with Christ's crucifixion. The same Lullington church that previously called to mind the poet's daughter now hosts 'Crucifixion, August, Lullington', in which 'the bleak orbit / of a whole culture adapts itself to hope'. Christian ritual is displaced to unfamiliar, inappropriate parts of the year: the final poem shifts the resurrection to a bleak January in Alnmouth. The speaker turns outward from a passionate late-night kiss to the viciousness of winter's beauty. The closing nothingness is provisional, a 'heaven where there is no night, & no dawn?', and a subscript fragment, '*The bright steel of your power*', might describe that heaven or point forwards.

Martinez de las Rivas is not here to curry favour, as his excoriation of 'those popinjays, / so deep in theory, so ostentatiously tolerant' in 'To a Metropolitan Poet' makes abundantly clear; he reminds himself, 'You are not theirs, finally'. This insistent refusal of the politenesses of professionalisation will not be to everyone's taste, but his sights are set beyond the fleeting recognition of popularity. *Black Sun* is a serious, vital collection that reasserts the value of poetic form in making sense of the chaotic, decaying modern world.

The Same River Twice

Attar, *The Conference of the Birds* translated by Sholeh Wolpe (W.W. Norton) £20

Reviewed by IAN POPLE

The Conference of the Birds is one of those world masterpieces which many may well have heard of but few have read. Written by Attar, Sheikh Farid-Ud-Din who was born in the twelfth century in north-eastern Iran, it is, as Sholeh Wolpe claims in her introduction, 'an allegorical poem about our human struggle, both physical and spiritual', more especially 'the soul's search for meaning'.

Probably the most familiar translation is the one by Afkham Darbandi and Dick Davis published by Penguin in 1984. However, a brief glimpse at Amazon suggests that there are about half a dozen translations available, some of them much more recent. And Peter Brook, famously, toured a dramatisation of the text around rural villages in Africa in the eighties.

Perhaps the fact that *The Conference of the Birds* may remain on people's 'to read' list is due to its nature. It is not a conventional narrative in the way that the Greek epics are, at least on the surface. It does not contain tales of derring-do, with great heroes and famous battles. These might be reasons why so few translations of it have been attempted until recently; it simply has not captured the imagination. Why there are more recent translations is, possibly, down to greater familiarity and fascination with Sufism, in particular, as Sufism is manifested in the poetry of Rumi. One of the legends surrounding Attar is that he bounced the baby Rumi on his knee and predicted Rumi's greatness. And Sholeh Wolpe may well be correct about another reason why *The Conference of the Birds* has gone so unread. Its stories 'inhabit the imagination, and slowly over time, their wisdom trickles down into the heart.'

The book 'recounts the perilous journey of the world's birds to the peaks of Mount Qaf – a mythical mountain that wraps around the earth – in search of the mysterious Simorgh, their king'. Well, so says the publicity. And, up to a point, that's correct. The poem is divided into ten sections, most of which correspond to sections of the birds' journey. And there is an epilogue, in which the poet Attar speaks straight to camera as it were. Within the ten named sections, the birds squabble, speculate, leave the party, and generally expatiate, rendered in verse. Within the ten sections, there are 'descriptions' of seven valleys, which the birds must cross in order to reach Simorgh. These valleys are each an allegory; for example, Wolpe describes the first valley as, 'Valley of the Quest, where the Wayfarer begins by casting aside all dogma, belief and unbelief.' And within the sections, there are prose parables. Each named section begins with a con-tents list of both the birds' 'poems' and the parables in that section, the list itself broken down into sections, such as, 'weakness', 'sinful' and 'ambivalence'. This constant breaking down might make the overall book seem fragmented, or at least, very schematic. And it is testament to the genius of the original writer and to Sholeh Wolpe's skill as a translator, that the book does not seem either of these things.

However, it is clear that *The Conference of the Birds* is not a book to be pushed through in the hope of finding narrative themes or, even, momentum. Sholeh Wolpe's skillful and measured translation means that the text is one to which one needs to return, and with which to build up a kind of relationship; and such is, perhaps, the nature of a true epic. The birds have characters which accumulate through the course of the whole book; in particular, the Hoopoe, who is the *de facto* leader of the group. The nature of 'the soul's search for meaning' pervades the, sometimes, slightly oblique parables, in ways which it takes time to adjust to; well, perhaps for this rather 'westernised' reader. But *The Conference of the Birds* is a haunting, moving book brought to fresh life in Wolpe's nuanced and resonant translation.

Reading in the Open Air

Chris Torrance, *The Magic Door*
(Test Centre) £30

Reviewed by IAN BRINTON

The opening sentence of Charles Olson's *Call me Ishmael* is central to an understanding of the wide-ranging poetry written by Chris Torrance, British poet who was born in Edinburgh, raised in Surrey and who moved to an isolated cottage in the Upper Neath Valley in South Wales nearly fifty years ago: 'I take SPACE to be the central fact to man born in America, from Folsom cave to now. I spell it large because it comes large here. Large, and without mercy.'

Writing on the back cover of Torrance's first collection of poems, *Green, Orange, Purple, Red* (published by Andrew Crozier's Ferry Press in 1968), Lee Harwood had alerted readers to this poet's awareness of the outside world as we look from side to side, trying to take in every detail in the whole limitless visual experience waiting there. It comes therefore as no surprise that the dedicatory lines at the opening of Book One of *The Magic Door* should refer to Harwood, amongst other poets 'opening each other's doors'. Throughout the four-hundred pages of this new publication of a major cycle of poems British poets rub shoulders with phantasmagorical appearances from Welsh mythological history; Iain Sinclair and Barry MacSweeney share ground with the kingdom of Brychein-iog as Chris Torrance's imaginative vision ranges from a world of the 'Celtic Church cut off from Rome 150 years / on the Western fringes of the dissociating empire' to his own residence in the house of stone 'stuck / like a worn & stubborn thumb / in the Glen of Mercury'. The poet's vision and transformation of reality ranges from his awareness of the roadside stones, evidence of the leakage of hermetic ideas 'filtered up from the Med', to his perception of the wind-stripped corpse of the dog-fox:

> hindquarters bared by weeks of galewash
> the naked balls hanging pathetic between
> thighs holed by death-blow or carrion creature.

Following on from the opening book, *Acrospirical Meanderings in a Tongue of the Time*, the five volumes which make up the sequence of *The Magic Door* offer insights into a precise nature of sensual intensity and Phil Maillard's finely judged introduction alerts us to the vivid existence of a poet who inhabits 'borders and boundaries' and whose Janus-like 'Magic Door' opens both outwards and inwards. As readers of this compelling cycle we become increasingly aware of how an exact understanding of weather and landscape becomes a reflection of the poet's self-knowledge: Chris Torrance lives *within* his chosen SPACE. He becomes increasingly aware of how the naming of things bestows a measure of power and yet how an isolated existence within a rural landscape opens up 'gulfs':

> that you knew were there
> & each time
> the pain of reaching
> seems to be more

Alongside his respect for the poetry of the so-termed 'New British Poets' (Crozier, Harwood, Roy Fisher, Haslam, Catling and Sinclair) Chris Torrance's work reveals a close understanding of the importance of Donald Allen's seminal volume from 1960, *The New American*

Poetry. The significance of this American backdrop was emphasised in a letter he wrote some fourteen years ago suggesting that, 'Yes, I grabbed onto Olson mid-6os, pored over the poetics... I hoovered up most of the *NAP 45–60* poets with enthusiasm & can point to bits of style and approach that I deliberately rehearsed & reworked in my early notebooks'. That letter concluded with an awareness of S P A C E : 'I've kept at Olson ever since. I love to take the big books outside in the summer, read those wide poems out in the open where they belong.'

Second Nature

Yvonne Reddick, *Ted Hughes: Environmentalist and Ecopoet* (Palgrave Macmillan), £79.99

Reviewed by D A V I D T R O U P E S

Everyone knows that Ted Hughes wrote about nature. His reputation rests on poems about hawks and pikes, salmon and jaguars, and the Yorkshire landscapes of his youth. His earliest critical exegetes, most notably the late Keith Sagar, tended to frame his work in anthropological terms, looking, for instance, to Jungian notions of the unconscious and the shamanistic religions of indigenous peoples to explain Hughes's project. Hughes himself, in letters, interviews and prose publications, encouraged this approach.

Hughes died in 1998, and the years since then have seen the worlds of ecopoetry and ecocriticism blossom, as the extent of our spoilage of the earth reveals itself, and artists and critics alike struggle toward an adequate response. Hughes was surely ahead of his time in this regard, but critical commentaries on his work have, to a large degree, remained bounded by the terms of those original, canonical exegetes. The effect of this has been to create the sense that Hughes's poetry is somehow dislocated in time, more an extended riff on Robert Graves's *The White Goddess* than a body of work responsive to the incipient environmental crisis during which it was written.

In *Ted Hughes: Environmentalist and Ecopoet*, Yvonne Reddick sets out to correct this, with a study which is nothing if not utterly thorough. Early chapters would serve well as a general introduction to Hughes's work in their detailed exploration of literary influences and themes, including accounts of Hughes's boyhood moorland tramping, his adventures through the post-industrial environments of Mexborough, and his singular university reading habits. Reddick is equally assiduous in laying out the development of ecocritical thought and ecopoetic practice in recent decades, allowing a side-by-side mapping of Hughes's poetry to this surge in literary eco-structures.

Many critics, of course, have written about the environmentalist and ecocritical aspects of Hughes's work, but Reddick's innovation is to situate each of Hughes's books in the politics, events and literature of its day, thereby avoiding the sort of long-view critical syntheses which help create the myth of a hermetic poet more interested in witchdoctors and goddess figures than in fishing treaties and nuclear fallout. The apocalyptic waste-scapes of *Crow*, for instance, written in the countercultural heyday of the 1960s, are explored as expressions of Hughes's and Plath's shared anxieties over the dangers of nuclear power. (Indeed, one of the book's strengths is its curiosity about the degree to which Hughes's thinking on environmental matters, and their translation into poetry, may have been influenced by Plath.) Ecocritical theories about 'occult toxicity networks' and 'waste studies', meanwhile, open up *Crow* as a more environmentally and politically engaged text than its mythic surface might suggest, allowing Hughes's esoteric poetry the opportunity to speak to newer generations of ecopoets.

Close textual readings are backed up by biographical accounts of Hughes's involvement with the public side of the environmental movement, including hitherto unaccounted activities, such as his co-founding and co-editing of the magazine *Your Environment* – activities which blossomed when Hughes took up the role of Poet Laureate. Along the way, Reddick avails herself of the wealth of archival material which has become available to researchers since Hughes's death: reading notes, unpublished letters and draft compositions provide new insights into Hughes's poetic method and the breadth of his autodidactic environmentalism. In his spirited defence of Devon's rivers, a battle against pollution he waged in newspapers and public hearings, we see Hughes at his most vocal and animated. That this struggle should intersect with his celebrated collection *River*, which Reddick calls 'the acme of Hughes's ecopoetic career', illustrates how his work is motivated as much by local political realities as by Jungian longing for psychic restitution.

Reddick remains alert to Hughes's potential for self-contradiction, especially regarding the ethics of fishing, hunting and trapping – activities which fostered and maintained his love of the outdoors and sense of natural connectivity, but to whose cruelties he was scarcely blind. This book is sometimes a study of the poetry and sometimes a study of the poet, and in both modes it succeeds at explaining why Hughes's work continues to feel so vital, and so prescient.

—————————— SOME CONTRIBUTORS ——————————

Rebecca Foster is an American freelance writer and proofreader based in the UK. Her book reviews and articles have been featured in the *Times Literary Supplement*, Literary Hub, the *Los Angeles Review of Books* and the *Pittsburgh Post-Gazette*. **Claudine Toutoungi**'s poems have appeared in *Poetry* (Chicago), *The Guardian*, *The Financial Times*, *Magma* and *The North*. Her debut collection is *Smoothie* (Carcanet, 2017). She also writes for theatre and radio. **Betsy Rosenberg**'s selected poems *A Future More Vivid* (Sheep Meadow Press, 2014) is forthcoming in dual language format, Hebrew-English, with Carmel Publishing House in Jerusalem. **Sophie Hannah**

is an internationally best-selling writer of psychological crime fiction, published in thirty-two languages and fifty-one territories. She has also published three novels featuring Agatha Christie's Hercule Poirot and five collections of poetry. **Nicholas Murray**'s most recent poetry collection is *The Museum of Truth* (Melos, 2018). He lives in rural Powys where, with his wife Susan, he runs the poetry imprint Rack Press. **Vona Groarke**'s seventh poetry collection *Double Negative* is due from Gallery Press next year. Her *Selected Poems* won the 2017 Pigott Prize. She teaches at the University of Manchester and, this winter, will be a Cullman Fellow at the New York Public Library. **Angela Leighton**'s most recent publications are *Spills* (Carcanet 2016), *Five Poems* (Clutag Press 2018) and *Hearing Things: The Work of Sound in Literature* (Harvard 2018). **Gregory O'Brien** is a poet and visual artist currently living in Central Otago, New Zealand. His most recent collection is *Whale Years* (Auckland University Press 2015). **Peter Vernon** was lecturer and visiting professor contracted by the British Council; his last appointment was at the University of Tours. He is currently writing a monograph on Joseph Conrad. **Ian Pople**'s *from The Evidence* is published by Melos Press. **Philip Armstrong** teaches in the English Department at the University of Canterbury in New Zealand. His most recent book is *Sheep* (Reaktion 2016). **Drew Milne**'s collected poems, *In Darkest Capital*, were published by Carcanet in 2017. *Third Nature* is forthcoming from Dostoevsky Wannabe in 2019. He is a Fellow of Corpus Christi College, Cambridge. **Mark Prendergast** is a poet living in Melbourne. His poems have been published in various journals including *Overland*, *Rabbit* and *foam:e*. **David Troupes** recently completed his PhD on Ted Hughes and Christianity, and a book with that title is under contract with Cambridge University Press. **Hal Coase** is a playwright and dramaturg. His most recent work, a stage adaptation of Virginia Woolf's *Mrs Dalloway*, opens at the Arcola Theatre in September. He is currently studying poetry at the University of Manchester. **Clare Jones** is the recipient of a grant from the Fulbright Program and an Alberta Metcalf Kelly

Fellowship from the Iowa Writers' Workshop. **Ian Brinton**'s recent publications include an edition of the *Selected Poems of John Riley* (Shearsman), *For the Future*, a festschrift for J. H. Prynne's eightieth birthday (Shearsman) and translations from the French of Philippe Jaccottet (Oystercatcher). **Joe Carrick-Varty** is a writer based in Manchester currently finishing his masters at the Center for New Writing. A winner of the 2017/18 New Poets Prize, his debut pamphlet is forthcoming (2019) with The Poetry Business. **Susan de Sola** recently won the Frost Farm Prize. Her poetry collection *Frozen Charlotte* is forthcoming in 2019. **Andrew Hadfield** is Profesor of English at the University of Sussex. He is the author of *A Cultural History of Lying: From the Oath of Supremacy to the Oath of Allegiance* (OUP, 2017) and is working on a book on class and literature. **Sam Trainor** is a Birmingham poet and a lecturer in Translation Studies at the Université de Lille. His latest translation is *Darker Shades: Imaging Others in Early Modern Art* by Victor Stoichita (Reaktion Books, 2018). **Bedilu Wakjira** is associate professor of linguistics at Addis Ababa University. He has published a novel, short stories, essays and three collections of poetry including *Fekat Nafeqiwoch* (*Those who long for spring*) and *Yetesfa Kitbat* (*The Hope Vaccine*). **A. E. Stallings** is an American poet and translator who has lived in Greece since 1999. Her verse translation of Hesiod's *Works and Days* is recently out with Penguin Classics, and she has a new volume of poetry, *Like*, forthcoming in the autumn with Farrar, Straus and Giroux. **Yasser Khanjer** was born in 1977 in the occupied Golan Heights. He was imprisoned in his early twenties for resistance to the occupation, and his first book was published while he was behind bars. **Fadwa Suleiman** was a Syrian actor, poet, and figure of the resistance. She left a stage career to join the peaceful opposition in Homs in 2011, and was obliged to flee Syria the following year. She published her first book in Arabic while in exile in France. Marilyn Hacker's English translations have also appeared in *POEM* and *Modern Poetry in Translation*. **Jena Schmitt** lives in Sault Ste. Marie, Ontario, Canada, with her family.

COLOPHON

Editors
Michael Schmidt (General)
Andrew Latimer (Deputy)

Editorial address
The Editors at the address on the right. Manuscripts cannot be returned unless accompanied by a stamped addressed envelope or international reply coupon.

Trade distributors
NBN International
10 Thornbury Road
Plymouth PL6 7PP, UK
orders@nbninternational.com

Design
Luke Allan
Typeset by Andrew Latimer in Arnhem Pro.

Represented by
Compass IPS Ltd
Great West House
Great West Road, Brentford
TW8 9DF, UK
sales@compass-ips.london

Copyright
© 2018 Poetry Nation Review
All rights reserved
ISBN 978-1-78410-154-1
ISSN 0144-7076

Subscriptions (6 issues)
INDIVIDUALS (print and digital):
    £39.50; abroad £49.00
INSTITUTIONS (print only): £56.00;
    abroad £70.00
INSTITUTIONS (digital):
    subscriptions from Exact Editions
    (https://shop.exacteditions.com/
    gb/pn-review)
to: *PN Review*, Alliance House
30 Cross Street, Manchester
M2 7AQ, UK

Supported by